Brazilian Jiu-Jitsu

Championship
TECHNIQUES

**Jean Jacques
Machado**

with
Kid Peligro

INVISIBLE CITIES PRESS • MONTPELIER, VERMONT

Invisible Cities Press
50 State Street
Montpelier, VT 05602
www.invisiblecitiespress.com

Library of Congress Cataloging-in-Publication Data
Machado, Jean Jacques.
Brazilian jiu-jitsu : championship techniques / Jean Jacques Machado with
Kid Peligro.
p. cm.
ISBN 1-931229-37-6
1. Jiu-jitsu--Brazil. 2. Jiu-jitsu--Training. I. Peligro, Kid. II.
Title.
GV1114.M338 2004
796.815'2--dc22
2004020305

Anyone practicing the techniques in this book does so at his or her own risk. The authors and the publisher assume no responsibility for the use or misuse of information contained in this book or for any injuries that may occur as a result of practicing the techniques contained herein. The illustrations and text are for informational purposes only. It is imperative to practice these holds and techniques under the strict supervision of a qualified instructor. Additionally, one should consult a physician before embarking on any demanding physical activity.

Printed in the United States of America

Book design by Peter Holm, Sterling Hill Productions

CONTENTS

Jean Jacques celebrates another win at the Black Belt Challenge.

Marcelo Alonso/O Tatame photo

give them incentive to pursue their goals. However, he has never considered himself different, thanks in great part to his family. Inside the family nucleus, they created a sense of normalcy that carried over into the larger world. Viewing himself as exactly like everyone else, he simply always strived to be the best.

It is easy for many people to find an excuse for failure or an excuse for failing even to try. It is much easier to say "I couldn't do it because I am slow, or old or weak" than to go out and accomplish something, but the difference is that when you set out to accomplish something and you achieve your goal, you get a great sense of doing! And it carries you forward and on to other accomplishments. Don't look for excuses, look for ways to accomplish your objectives!

Difficulties present themselves in all aspects of life, not only the physical world. And people sometimes create obstacles that do not really exist as a way to justify failure! Champions, however, see difficulties as opportunities to be faced and know that you always evolve when you face and conquer challenges. Conquering increasingly difficult challenges helps you grow. Your knowledge expands and the internal satisfaction of achieving something is greater each time.

Of course, you don't always win, but sometimes out of the biggest failures you get the biggest evolutions.

All kinds of people come to my academy, and if they are slow or fat or old or stiff and they ask me if they can succeed, I tell them, Of course! It will take commitment and open-mindedness and some adaptation. But this is part of the beauty and art of jiu-jitsu: It is not that you are going to have to adapt to the techniques, but rather that the techniques are going to adapt to your body and to you. Regardless of size or athletic condition, all my students can achieve the same objectives. Some may get there faster and some slower, but we all are going to get there if we stick to it. I may show a technique to fifty different people, and each one interprets it and adjusts it in his own way and brings it back to me with unique nuances and shades. That is one of the best things about jiu-jitsu: you do not have to be an athlete to be good!

Todd Nathanson, a first-degree Black Belt instructor at the academy, adds:

> **Besides being a teacher, Jean Jacques is an excellent role model— beyond jiu-jitsu. Watch the way he conducts himself with his family, in his business, and in athletics. But he's also an excellent teacher. What he facilitates most is a structure in which you can grow your own techniques. You are not confined to what he does or what he teaches, but rather he allows your jiu-jitsu to flourish in its own manner. He will teach you a basic technique and then allow your body or athletic ability to determine what form of the technique you will actually use. He then molds and finesses what you have. He tweaks and he corrects what you have.**

Of course, the more dedicated (and most athletic) people will always improve more quickly. If you put two students against each other, and one trains and tries hard all the time, and the other never trains and doesn't pay attention when they fight each other, the more dedicated student will always win. In most martial arts, the greatest benefit people derive is self-improvement: they lose weight, they change their eating habits, they dedicate themselves to bettering themselves. This is even truer if you are pursuing the championship: if you dedicate yourself to improving your performance, you will better your life as well!

Tournament Preparation

How long before a tournament should you begin preparing? The answer depends on your maintenance level of fitness. Of course, not everyone has the luxury to maintain the level that Jean Jacques and John Machado do, but athletes serious about competition should be training regularly and be basically fit. Given this condition, Jean Jacques generally recommends that you give yourself three months to prepare physically, mentally, and spiritually to perform at your greatest proficiency.

Physical Preparation

To help them prepare physically, Jean Jacques encourages students to decrease their outside work and other forms of recreation. If you like to play softball a few times a week, for example, you might take a three-month break to concentrate solely on your goal of performing well at the upcoming event. Jean Jacques himself begins by diminishing his outside load, teaching less and training more. He turns his classes over to an assistant, so that he can train in the class as if he were a regular student. Additionally, he trains before class with a workout of some sort, perhaps weights or cardio.

When people ask me who I train with, I tell them I train with my students. They keep me in shape. Often, I will work myself very hard before I train with my students to push myself more. I do a lot of tests: sometimes I train when I'm very tired and see the results; other times I do the reverse, training fresh, then working out to push my conditioning that way. I imagine the worst conditions I can and try to replicate them. For example, I might imagine a difficult competition situation and then focus on that situation with every student in my class. Sometimes there are thirty or more, and I will decide that I HAVE TO SUBMIT all of them. I will start with the least experienced and work toward the most adept. Even when I am tired, I will stop only after I have submitted all of them. This prepares me both physically and mentally. Imagine that in a fight I realize I am tired. Immediately, I can recall that I trained with thirty students when I was tired to begin with, and I still submitted them all, so I cannot be tired now! This is the mental component to my physical training: I tell myself that I am going to do something and I will do it. Even if I lose a leg or an arm, I am going to finish the task!

A note to the wise: It is also important not to overtrain. If you train too much, you begin to get injured and then all your preparation is for naught. Better to spend time thinking about the match, but not put in too much extra time on the mat. You just might leave everything on the mat and have nothing left over for the fight!

Mental and Spiritual Preparation

Obviously, it is almost impossible not to sharpen both your physical and your mental abilities at the same time if you do things right! However, training is often very solitary and it is difficult to train and work out alone. Sometimes you will have training partners, but often they are not going to compete or they don't have the same commitment as you do, so a time will come when you surpass their dedication and it will be just you against yourself, trying to push your limits.

To build your mental stamina under these circumstances, you need to keep your training fresh—even surprising. Whether you are going to hit the weights or going for a cardio conditioning, set the goals, force yourself to do things, and test yourself! That is a way to find out your limits, and your mental and spiritual muscles will get stronger as you use them to make you train even when you don't want to.

Sometimes I get up at 4 a.m. to work out. Other times, my trainer calls me at home at 11 p.m. and says, "Hey, we are going to work out!" I grunt, but I go because we have made a pact ahead of time that he is going to push my limits and test my resolve. Except for meal time, my schedule is at his mercy. The question must be: "Do I really want to win?" And my answer must always be "Yes!" If I waiver, then I must reach deeper to find strength inside to continue. It is a personal challenge that I make, to be ready at all times and at any time! This fortifies the mind and the spirit.

Mental support is also a part of any training program. Having someone there encouraging you and correcting you is not only a great thing, but a necessary one. Jean Jacques knows you can't do it alone.

Very few people are able to survive on their own. It is important for a competitor to have a good academy, one that supports his goals and objectives. Your instructor and teammates should be an asset to your preparation.

As Todd Nathanson states:

Jean Jacques loves competition, and he encourages everybody to compete. But whether you compete or not, we are all part of the same family in the academy, and we all help that one person or team achieve their objective. If that person wins, then it becomes a victory for the entire academy and for everyone else who has helped the person in any way, be it on the mat or just being a friend. We are an entire family and team pushing each individual to the victory.

Technical Preparation

When people ask Jean Jacques what his favorite move is, he replies that he doesn't have one. Instead, he has a little circle of three, four, or sometimes more positions that he can execute effectively in any given situation.

For instance, if I want to sweep someone, I may work on three to four minutes' worth of sequenced techniques to attempt to get leverage here and there. I cannot even feel what I am doing because it is automatic, but I have a strong conviction that one of the techniques in the sequence is going to sweep the opponent. These movements are so interlocked that they are like a powerful vitamin that has been put together over many, many years to deliver just the right combination of parts to achieve a desired goal.

Todd Nathanson adds that the best piece of advice he ever received from Jean Jacques concerned the circles and combinations of techniques:

He told me about becoming trapped within a certain circle of techniques that you know very well. He said that sometimes you must expand from that core group into a larger circle of techniques, some that you are not so proficient in. At any given time, you use a particular set of techniques that work, and every so often you must step out of that comfort zone to work on other moves, some of which may continuously fail you. Once those start to work, you have a new circle and it is time to expand that new circle.

John Machado working the half-guard game.
John Machado Personal Archives photo

Of course, no matter what your skill level, you have your "own" positions, the ones that you have extreme confidence in executing effectively. The key is to evolve to a place in your training to the point that you have this same level of confidence in your execution of all techniques—at all times, in any situation. Of course, that point remains very distant for many years for most competitors. But there are shortcuts to getting there, and competing is one of them.

Drills

Some of the most important items in this book are the drills. If you want to progress quickly and become successful both in school and in competition, your movements and reactions must become automatic.

The main objective of each drill is to have an exercise that replicates a movement that occurs in jiu-jitsu so you can repeat it over and over until it becomes automatic. In a sparring match, a casual training session, or a match in a tournament, positions happen infrequently or frequently, without a pattern or our control. If you want to practice a sweep, for instance, you can't rely on sparring and competition; you either have to get a partner who is willing to help you repeat the same movement over and over (and that is often difficult) or figure out a method of practicing the motion alone.

In this book, Jean Jacques presents a series of one-person and two-person drills. He has chosen exercises that replicate positions that happen frequently. Practicing these drills will greatly speed your progress and turbo-charge your execution, improving your accuracy and technical mastery of that move and reducing the time it takes for you to apply the technique effectively.

Drills are also a great and fun way to sharpen your techniques. Much like sharpening a sword, drills really do sharpen your movements. Many fighters don't like drills and that is fine if you are a natural athlete, but if you are not, drills are critical. A great benefit of drills is the ability to develop your timing so when the position actually occurs, you execute it right away— sharply, effectively, and correctly. And that can be the difference between winning and losing!

Techniques

The techniques presented here will expand your circle of moves. These are techniques especially selected by Jean Jacques to give you escapes, reversals, or attacks from the many situations that occur in a fight.

A note about submissions: Jean Jacques predicates his game and his competition strategy on winning by submission. In order to do that, you should first and foremost know the submissions. But second, you need to be in control of the match, so you can apply the submission. Of course, it's also true that many times you will be so far behind on points that the only way to win the match is with a submission. So Jean Jacques demonstrates many of his favorite submissions from many different positions. When mastered, these techniques—combined with the ones he presented in his previous book, *Black Belt Techniques*—will put your competition game into overdrive and make you a submission threat from every position.

Getting Your Game

Before a tournament, however, is not the time to adjust your game; before the tournament is the time to practice what you do best and to develop your confidence in, knowledge of, and execution of your best positions. As teachers, both Jean Jacques and his brother, John Machado, create opportunities for each student competitor to play his game and develop it solidly. Jean Jacques:

> **Learning new techniques and positions before competition will lead to doubt and indecision. In competition, you need confidence, certainty, and instantaneous reactions. You shouldn't be thinking, "I am not good at this sweep." When you add a new element to your game, you throw your old game out of whack, and it takes time to fit all the parts into a new whole. This process occurs faster with some than with others, but it takes even more time before the new move becomes a reflex. If you have to think about it at all, your opportunity to use it will probably have passed. Moves must be instantaneous reflexes, executed before you know why you are executing them. Just as when you touch a hot iron, your reflexes yank your hand away! If you were to think, "This iron is hot, if I leave my hand in contact with it I will get burned, I need to take my fingers away," you would have a third-degree burn. The speed of reaction is much faster than the thought! The same is true of your positions and reactions: they need to be reactive decisions, not thinking decisions.**

The more reactive you are, the more you will also begin to predict your opponent's intentions. How many times have you thought about doing something only to have your opponent counter it almost before you start! Jean Jacques always tells his students that the worst part in training is the beginning, because they learn the positions and then train with more advanced athletes who react correctly to every technique. Nothing works, because the advanced athletes know what is going to happen. But after many repetitions, the beginners start to get the timing of the position, and after they get the timing, pieces fall together. When you go into competitions, you want to go in with techniques you already know work.

I put my students in adverse positions and have them practice getting to those positions in which they have confidence. If, for instance, you like to play from the top and pass the guard, I may start your opponent on your back and ask you to show me how you will get back to where you want to be. We would then drill this technique until you are comfortable that you can deal with it in a match. I would also tell you that you have to play "your" music; if your opponent is trying to play "his" music, you have to play louder and overcome his tune!

No matter how you teach, students will adjust to your style. Mine inevitably end up emphasizing submissions, and I always stress enjoying themselves during competition. But the real key before competition is to emphasize what you do best and how to get there from anywhere.

No way out! Jean Jacques weaves his spider web around Tsuyoshi Kosaka, ADCC 2001 Absolute.
ADCC Archives/Mike McNeil photo

John Machado prepares his students with a similar concern for emphasizing their strengths:

> When I am preparing anyone for competition, the first thing I want to know is what kind of conditioning the athlete is in, how long he has to prepare, and what type of game he has. Is it fast? Slow? Then I try to identify the strongest part of his game. Mike Tyson had that left hook that made him famous. Everyone knew it was his punch, but he still was able to deliver it. Similarly, I look for the student's greatest strength and tell him that it is going to be his ace, to keep it up his sleeve.

Naturally, the student still needs to have a solid sweep, a certain takedown, or even a submission. He needs certain positions that will get him the points or out of predicaments. And he needs to have a favorite submission ready—it could be a footlock, a choke from the guard, or any trustworthy technique. He will fight the entire fight with that at the ready. Of course, at the highest level, you need to have more than just that, but until you get there this is the best route to success. John continues:

> Next we determine whether the student has a top game or a bottom game. If he has a strong wrestling or judo background, then I suggest the game should be from the top. If he is better at takedowns, then we need to explore that. We make a game plan to fit the style. We tell him, "You are going to take him down and then do this, this, and this." This method worked with Ricco Rodrigues, who at the time had only three months of jiu-jitsu and became World Champion and then ADCC Champion. We gave him a basic game that took advantage of his strengths: his size and his takedown skills. We told him "Ricco, you are going to take the opponent down, smother him down. If you get in the guard you should stick one arm inside the legs (which is risky because it gives the opponent an opportunity for the triangle); when your opponents slap the triangle on you, you just bend them back. Use your 280 pounds to smother them more and pass the guard!" What a perfect plan for a beginner! That plan would not work, of course, if you are a lightweight. In that case, you must have a good guard. We build our game plan around existing strengths.

There is an effective game plan for everyone. If you are a beginner, you have one plan; if you are intermediate, your game is another; and if you are advanced, your game is yet another. Everything depends on your conditioning, your athletic ability, and your technical skills, of course, but you also have the basic principles to guide you: bring the game to your arena, know your limitations (be they conditioning, flexibility, technical knowledge, physical strength), and know your assets—the "ace in the hole" submission that works for you most of the time, that good sweep that you pull off with just about anyone, or that guard pass that is very effective. With those techniques in hand, you can go into the fight looking for the spots or leading the match toward spots where you can use them. And when the opportunity comes, make sure you use them effectively!

Competition Strategy

Jean Jacques

When Jean Jacques competes, he tries to control the match at all times. If you have control of the match, you should be ahead in points as well. There are many fighters who win by knowing the rules of the event and adhering tightly to the scoring opportunities.

> **Athletes need to know the rules of the event, but I don't base my fighting on the rules. Realistically, my strategy may not be the best because today's level of play makes it hard for one fighter to submit the other. However, the way I see it, and with the level of confidence that I have in myself, there's no reason not to go for the kill. I always go for the knockout. In looking for the knockout, you should be in advantage to your adversary in relation to points no matter what the rules are. But even if I am behind 10-to-0 with one minute to go in the match, in my mind I know I will submit my adversary before the fight is over.**

Jean Jacques's confidence and reputation have a tangible effect on his matches:

> **It is very difficult to explain, but one of the best feelings is when I face an opponent and I see in his face the fear of sub-mission. I can read what they are thinking: "I may be able to beat Jean Jacques, but I run the risk of being submitted!" I like seeing that he is worried. In BJJ, losing by points is one thing,**

being submitted is another, completely different outcome. It strikes fear in people, giving me an initial advantage. It gives me pleasure to feel the confidence that if my opponent escapes, I am going for it.

Jean Jacques tries to convey the same philosophy to his students, teaching them to go for the submission and give credit to their opponent if at the end they didn't achieve their objective.

The moment you go into a match worried about your opponent, you are at a disadvantage and are better off going home. The fight is the time to have extreme confidence in your game. I want my opponents to be thinking: "Darn, Jean Jacques is in my bracket. He is a tough nut to crack. I better be careful or I am going to be submitted!" I try to make sure the fear is justified. That is part of the physical, technical, spiritual, and mental part of training that I got from my instructors, Carlos Gracie Jr. and Rickson. I was taught to look for submissions from any position, to find a way or look for a way to submit the opponent no matter what position I was in. Carlinhos also teaches this philosophy, but students don't so much learn this approach as absorb it from their instructor's example.

Naturally, no student will turn out a carbon copy of his instructor; there will be appropriate differences stemming from each student's adaptations of techniques. Yet it's true that the way an instructor thinks and reacts, and his philosophy of training and fighting, simply percolate to his students. All the more reason to keep things simple:

The simpler things are, the more effective they are. If you look at today's fights, you'll see that there really aren't new positions but rather old positions recycled in new ways. Some positions become everyday techniques, everyone gets used to defending them, so the position falls into disuse for a few years. Then people forget how to use it and defend it, and someone brings it back, perhaps with a slightly different twist. Although everyone may be amazed, the fact is that most positions have been explored. They just drift off the map from time to time.

John Machado

John prefers a different type of game than his brother:

I love the way Jean Jacques fights and trains, with a lot of movement and always on the go. I liken him to a cat moving on the mat. But I also believe that everyone is an individual, and everyone has to have his own style. My style is more deliberate. I like to smother the opponent and make smaller gains and valorize each position. I can and will go fast, but I prefer to give every position its due. I have a game of patience; I believe everything has to be done for a reason. I prefer to wait for my opponent to give me something that I want, rather than just forcing the issue.

John believes in submissions as well. His record as a competitor has a large percentage of his wins by submission, but when it comes to competition, he has a different vision.

The tournament these days is a sporting event first of all. Scoring is very important. A tournament is nothing more, nothing less than a game. Its goal is not necessarily to determine the best martial artist on the street but rather to identify the one who is more capable of navigating the tournament rules and environment. You should be in the best conditioning you can be, have a tight game where you know what you like at all times. And the match may be decided by a single sweep or a position that will decide the match. Nowadays the athletes are very well prepared, especially in the conditioning part, so if you want to win at every level you need to pay attention to that.

John understands clearly that athletes are very well prepared, especially physically, so competitors who want to win at every level must pay attention to conditioning. However, he also believes that regardless of your fitness, you still have a lot to gain by entering in competition. He says:

I have fought many times when I was ill, or didn't have the chance to properly prepare. When that is the case, I had to change my strategy and I learned a lot about competing every time. Also, jiu-jitsu is a martial art dedicated to self-defense, and you just don't know when you are going to be required to use it for that purpose. If the occasion arises where you must defend yourself, you cannot simply excuse yourself because you may be tired or sick. Entering a tournament in less than ideal conditioning has, in fact, some advantages: If you are not in good shape, then you need to fight a lot smarter. You have to slow the game down, find places to rest and recoup your energies. You should have those places already mapped in your head, positions where you are very comfortable and that you can control with less effort. Whether you rest in the side control or in the guard, you need to be able to get there, recoup, and wait for your opponent to make a mistake.

John believes that everyone should compete at least once, but of course he doesn't force anyone. Tournaments do allow martial artists to come as close to real fighting as they can without undue violence.

Always creating, Jean Jacques sets up a sweep and a submission against Ricardo Arona, ADCC Absolute Finals 2001.
ADCC Archives/Mike McNeil photo

If someone approaches me and says he wants to compete and wants my help, I try to demystify what a tournament is: a tournament is nothing special. It is a test, nothing more, nothing less. The next step is to determine his objectives in competing: does he want to just participate in this tournament or to be a local champion, a state champion, or a World Champion? How much he wants to do determines the length of the plan that we are going to implement, and our short- and long-term goals.

John also stresses the importance of the emotional aspect of competition: the more you can control that emotional side, the better you will compete. If you get mad because you lost or blame the referee, you are wasting both needed energy and the opportunity to grow as a fighter. If you can go into a match without any emotion, then you are halfway to victory. Of course, that is very difficult and comes usually only with experience.

Ideally, you should get to the point where going into a match feels the same as sparring at the academy, where you should generally be relaxed and train without any emotion at all. You think clearly, and there is no pressure on you to perform. Consequently, the result of the training session is irrelevant in your mind. It should be the same in competition. The key difference is to try to focus whatever excitement and adrenaline you have going into sharpness—and save some for extra fuel for your stamina. If you let your emotions control you, you will spend a lot of energy without any return. Even if you are the best-prepared fighter in the universe, if you can't control your nerves you may just spend all that energy worrying about fighting rather than applying it in the fight itself.

You must also keep in mind that the referee may not always score the way you expect. You need to learn not to despair and to remain unaffected by the referee. Concentrate on what you can control and continue with your game plan. It will be very hard for you to fight against your opponent when you are worrying about the refereeing. The pace of your fighting is also a critical element of competition style. John:

Frequent Flyer miles anyone? John Machado elevates another victim for an overhead sweep, Sombo Championships.

John Machado Personal Archives photo

You can be prepared for a twelve-round boxing bout, but if you use all that energy in the first minute and have nothing left in the tank for the other rounds, you will have a long fight ahead. You develop your pace by competing often, by having a strategy so that you are prepared for what is happening, and by not wasting a lot of energy dealing with surprises.

The match is a game. It is you against the opponent, against the clock, sometimes against the referee. You have to demonstrate to the referee that you are achieving your positions, you have to keep an eye on the scoring, you have to listen to your coaches. You have to learn to play this game and still be able to focus on the job at hand of winning the match. Only by competing often will you become better at the game and learn to conform to the rigors and demands of competition.

Match Time

The greatest challenge of competition is its limited time. You have to learn your opponent's game, adjust to it, and impose your game in what seems like no time at all. The athlete who wins is generally the one who can do these things the best. Some people are very good in the academy but don't perform or adjust well enough in tournaments. They aren't yet capable of achieving the rhythm that competition demands. They haven't mastered the process of imposing their games in the speed of competition. Adept as they may be, they end up falling into their opponent's game and losing the match. Sometimes it is only one or two positions that your opponent applies that cause you to fall behind and lose the ability to impose your game. Always be alert to time passing.

Dion Watts, a Jean Jacques purple belt, points out another aspect of the time limit:

> **Jean Jacques often tells us, "Sometimes you have to wait for your moment. Especially to escape certain positions! A lot of times you have to wait for your opponent to move first, to give you an escape!" Lower belts often get into a position and just want to get out again. We struggle and waste a lot of energy, and many times our haste causes us to give up or even to be submitted. Remembering Jean Jacques's words of advice has enabled me to wait for an opponent to move, then escape when opportunity comes—when I otherwise would have struggled haphazardly and opened myself up to attack.**

From First Competition to Championship

John Machado:

When a student of mine is about to enter his first competition, I don't require anything from him. I tell him he is entering this event to gain experience. The result is not important, but I want him to give his best. Whether you win or lose your first match is irrelevant; the important thing is to begin competing.

The mental part of competition is a huge portion of the whole equation, especially for beginning fighters. In your first few tournaments, just focus on gaining experience. Record all your fights and develop a fight library. Later in your life and career, you will wish you had the early matches on video, and you can review your fights to see the mistakes and the effective moves that you made. Watching not only allows you to relive the fight and gain extra insights, but it also enables you to calmly and unemotionally see the opportunities that presented themselves and the mistakes you made.

With experience, you inevitably gain confidence. It is like taking a test in school. If you fail, you take it again, and little by little you start to learn how to answer the questions more quickly, you start to learn to control your emotions, you don't get as nervous, and soon you are passing without problem. You get the quickness of thinking, very important in tournaments where you have a limited amount of time and very little chance to correct your mistakes.

After ten or twenty matches, you will be looking for additional information. You will know what is lacking in your game and will be ready to absorb new information like a sponge. John:

As an instructor, I can only give to the student what he can absorb, so I have to know when the student is ready for new information and how much he can take. I begin to adjust strategies and technical aspects after the student has been in ten or more matches and is psychologically stronger and knows what his basic strengths and weaknesses are. Then, after we feel he is ready, we can do more specific training. If he needs to work on takedowns, we may add a throw; if he needs a bottom game, then we will work on a sweep or a submission from the bottom. It is always important not to try to add too much to his game, which would set him back significantly. It is also important not to mess with his game when he is near a competition. At this point, less is more.

You never know what is going to happen in any fight, of course, but the more you know about yourself and your opponent the better. If, for example, you know he has a stronger stand-up game (he may be a wrestler or a good judo fighter), then you need to be prepared to pull guard or to take the match to the mat without being scored on. For each opponent, you will develop a different strategy, but it is important to remain open to unexpected openings and turns of events. Naturally, the more technical knowledge you have, the more options you possess, and conversely, the less you know, the fewer options you have. If you have only one submission, you will struggle much harder to get a submission than someone who has ten.

The more you fight the better. As you start to become a champion fighter, you should start selecting which tournaments you are going to fight in. At this point, your preparation will change because champions have more to lose than other competitors. You will have to prepare more and better so you can consistently fight at the level you expect of yourself. John:

A singular advantage of BJJ competitions is that you can have a hundred matches and your body will still be intact. You take the great no-holds-barred fighters of our time, Rickson for instance, and you see the impact on them. Royce's body, after he fought four UFCs, was suffering and he had to take time off before he could return. After just fifteen fights, a fighter in NHB is all damaged or spent, while a BJJ fighter can go on and on without that physical abuse on his body.

Note that there are generally two ways to start a match. Which you choose often depends on your stamina and conditioning. If you have great stamina, you may go directly for the attack; if you are not as well prepared, you may want to fight a more defensive fight. But, then again, you may also be in great shape and decide that you want to fight a tight defensive match to test your opponent's positions and his patience as well. Remember that you usually can study your opponent in the beginning of a match. If you have a five-minute fight, you still have four minutes to fight if you spend the opening minute analyzing your adversary. Or you can go all out and apply pressure from the beginning (even if your conditioning is not excellent) just to see how your opponent reacts to mayhem. In this case, however, remember to reserve a little energy for the final minutes.

Strategy Situations

Because so many matches are won or lost on points, serious competitors always know the score, always have a sense of the time remaining in the match, and adjust their strategies accordingly. Below, you will find some general strategy guidelines that take score and time into account. Naturally, any guideline should be broken if doing so will result in submitting your opponent.

Points Are Even

Early in the match: Try to set up or position yourself to achieve one of your strongest scoring moves, such as a sweep, reversal, or takedown. Feel your opponent's strengths and weaknesses. Don't take any risky chances at this stage and give your opponent an easy chance to score.

Middle of the match: If the score is still tied, it is time to attempt a low-risk attack or scoring move. Even if you fail and get behind in points, you still have time to recover.

Late in the match: This is the time to take fewer chances. The match may be decided on one advantage, and you want it to be on your behalf. Attempt solid moves that you believe have the highest chances of success. Remember that any attack, if not successful, opens the door for your opponent to score. Exception: If you are fighting someone who is much better than you, you may want to try to keep the score even and risk a scoring move late in the match for the win.

Behind on Points

Early in the match: Remember there is still time to recoup. Maintain your game strategy, and try to probe your opponent for openings. Take advantage of them without risking the big move.

Middle of the match: It may be time to take chances and push the game. If you are behind by a small number of points, say 2 or 3, stay within your game but increase the urgency. Attempt to score points from sweeps or guard passes (from the bottom or top). If you are behind by a large amount, it is time to start going for it. Look for submissions. Your opponent will probably be more cautious and risk less, so be ready to be aggressive and take bigger risks.

Late in the match: Again, if you are behind by 2 or 3 points late in the match, you must take risks. But don't panic! You can even the score with something as simple as a reversal followed by a knee-on-stomach (if on bottom) or by passing the guard (if on top). As time runs out, you need to take bigger risks. If you are behind by a large amount, it is time to throw caution to the wind and go for submissions.

Ahead on Points

Early in the match: Control the position and let your opponent open up. He is the one who has to take chances, not you. Be ready for this and advance your position when the opening occurs. If a submission option comes your way, this may be the time to take it. Don't relax and play safe, but don't take unnecessary chances. In any case, stay focused.

Middle of the match: At this point, your opponent is starting to panic and will take even bigger chances. Be ready for the improbable and take advantage of any openings, but do not risk a big move. Remember, you are ahead. A submission may come your way as your opponent takes more and more risks to reverse the score.

Late in the match: Your opponent will try to submit you. Be alert for foot and knee locks, as they can come at any time. At the same time, your opponent will have to take even bigger chances than these, yielding not only position but also submission opportunities. Stay very alert and don't give him a chance to submit you or to score points if the score is close.

Point-Scoring Positions

Jean Jacques and John know that submissions are final and they prefer to submit an opponent rather than win the match by points, however they both know that you cannot win every match by submission. The scoring system awards points for positions achieved and moves accomplished that signify an advancement in the fight. Understanding the scoring system is paramount if you intend to be successful in competition. Since most competitions are run under the International Brazilian Jiu-Jitsu Federation (IBJJF) rules, we have placed the IBJJF rules section in the appendix. Studying the rules and mastering their nuances and details will greatly help you to understand your goals and strategy in competition.

Takedown

Any type of knocking down or taking the opponent down on his backside, 2 points. If an athlete is thrown to the ground and does not land on his back, the thrower must pin his adversary to the ground in the same position for at least 3 seconds to gain the takedown points.

Passing the Guard

The athlete who is above his adversary or between his legs moves to his opponent's side and thereby establishes a perpendicular or longitudinal

position over his adversary's trunk—dominating him and leaving him no space to move or to escape the position, 3 points.

Note: If the athlete underneath avoids the move by getting to his knees or standing up, the initiative will not be awarded 3 points but will be awarded an advantage.

Knee-on-Stomach

The athlete on top places one knee on his adversary's stomach, with his other leg slightly flexed and foot planted on the ground holds his collar or sleeve and belt, 2 points.

Note: If the athlete underneath does not allow his adversary to bring his knee down onto

the belly and if the one on top does not establish the position completely, the move will not be awarded with 2 points but will be awarded an advantage.

The Mount

The athlete sits on his opponent's torso; the opponent can be lying on his stomach, side, or back, 4 points. The one mounted can be on top of one of his opponent's arms but never on both. It will also be considered a mount if he has one knee and one foot on the ground.

Note: No points will be awarded if the feet or knees of the athlete on top are not on the ground but on his opponent's leg. Also, if an athlete applies a triangle while in the guard and in so doing lands mounted on his opponent, the move will be considered a sweep, not a mount. (See Passing the Guard, above.)

Taking the Back

The athlete grabs his adversary's back, taking hold of his neck and wrapping his legs around his opponent's waist, with his heels leaning on the inner side of his opponent's thighs, prohibiting him from leaving the position, 4 points.

Note: The points will not be awarded if both heels are not properly positioned on the inner part of the adversary's thighs.

The Sweep

The athlete underneath has his opponent in his guard (in between his legs) or in the half-guard (having one of his adversary's legs between his) and is able to get on top of his adversary by inverting his position, 2 points.

MEET THE TEAM

The Authors

Jean Jacques Machado

Jean Jacques Machado was born in Rio de Janeiro, Brazil. Cousins to the Gracies, he and his brothers spent much of their childhood training alongside Royce, Royler, and the other future champions at the Gracie clan's home in the Teresopolis mountains. Jean Jacques trained with Rolls, Carlos Jr., and Rickson Gracie, receiving his black belt at the age of eighteen. He soon developed a reputation as the submissions specialist *par excellence*.

By the time Jean Jacques moved to America in 1992, he had won the biggest titles in Brazil and needed new challenges. His brothers were teaching in an academy in the Valley that they opened with Chuck Norris, and were also teaching out of their garage in Redondo Beach. Both academies started to grow, and then they exploded after Royce Gracie's victory in the first Ultimate Fighting Championship in 1993. Today Jean Jacques operates his own academy in Tarzana, California, where he trains some of the world's top champions, as well as the LAPD and Navy Seals.

In 1999 Jean Jacques was invited to compete in the pinnacle of submission wrestling events, the ADCC World Submission Wrestling Championships. In his international debut, he submitted all four of his opponents each in five minutes or less, a feat yet to be duplicated. He was runner-up in 2000 and runner-up in the absolute division in 2001, losing by points to an opponent forty-five pounds heavier. Of his eleven wins in three ADCC events, nine were by submission.

Kid Peligro

One of the leading martial arts writers in the world, Kid Peligro is responsible for regular columns in *Grappling* and *Gracie Magazine*, as well as one of the most widely read Internet MMA news pages, *ADCC News*. He has been the author or coauthor of an unprecedented string of bestsellers in recent years, including *The Gracie Way, Brazilian Jiu-Jitsu: Theory and Technique, Brazilian Jiu-Jitsu Self-Defense Techniques, Brazilian Jiu-Jitsu Black Belt Techniques, Brazilian Jiu-Jitsu Submission Grappling Techniques,* and *Superfit*. A black belt in jiu-jitsu, Kid's broad involvement in the martial arts has led him to travel to the four corners of the Earth as an ambassador for the sport that changed his life. He makes his home in San Diego.

The Advisor

John Machado

To help compile the techniques for this book, Jean Jacques chose his brother John. John's wealth of experience both teaching and competing, along with his expert understanding of the techniques, make him the perfect complement to Jean Jacques. John's deliberate and precise style differs from Jean Jacques's and provides another perspective for practitioners. John was the co-captain, along with his brothers, of the powerhouse Machado Competition team, which dominated the competition scene in the 1990s in the United States. With John's technical expertise and attention to strategy, the brothers were able to develop athletes from other grappling backgrounds into world champions with as little as three months of Brazilian jiu-jitsu instruction, simply by concentrating on a gameplan that took advantage of the fighters' backgrounds and natural abilities. John got his black belt at age nineteen. He started training with Crolin Gracie and then had a similar upbringing to Jean Jacques's, learning under Carlos Gracie Jr. and taking classes with Rickson Gracie for some time. He is a fourth-degree black belt with more than twenty years of martial arts experience. In addition to his multiple state, national, and international titles in Brazilian jiu-jitsu, he has been an actor or choreographer for many TV shows and movies, including *Walker, Texas Ranger, Kickboxer 4,* and *Under Seige 2.*

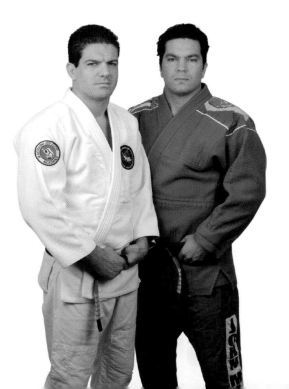

ONE-PERSON DRILLS

Instantaneous reactions are absolutely essential to the jiu-jitsu competitor. As noted earlier, the only way to develop your automatic responses is to practice moves and positions until they no longer are the consequence of a thought but are written in your muscles. One of the problems with progressing in jiu-jitsu is that while you need a partner to practice most of the moves, your partner is usually trying to stop you from completing the moves rather than helping you learn them. These one-person drills will allow you to train without the help of a partner and enable you to do the repetitions that you normally cannot do in a sparring match or in a class.

We recommend that you perform these drills as often as you can, of course, but especially before you train. Depending on your physical conditioning and time restraints, you may not want to do the entire set before every class. Therefore, you should break them down into several warm-up routines that can be used prior to training sessions. Note that your goals in drilling should be precision and technique first, not speed. Speed will come as a result of practice. Perform each drill at least 10 repetitions per side.

1

Standing up in base

Standing up in base is a very important technique not only for sports jiu-jitsu but also for submission grappling, No Holds Barred (NHB) competitions, and basic self-defense. By properly developing your ability to stand up in base, you will learn to balance your body in many ways, enabling you to avoid takedowns and sweeps. This drill will help you master this extremely important technique. Make sure you practice it slowly at first, feeling your body balance throughout the entire movement, and speed it up only as you master it.

1 Sit on the mat with your arms braced on the ground behind you. Your hands should be slightly further apart than shoulder width. Your knees should be slightly flexed and your feet firmly planted on the mat.

ONE-PERSON DRILLS ONE-PERSON DRILLS ONE-PERSON DRILLS ONE-PERSON DRILLS ON
DRILLS ONE-PERSON DRILLS ONE-PERSON DRILLS ONE-PERSON DRILLS ONE-PERSON DRILL
ONE-PERSON DRILLS ONE-PERSON DRILLS ONE-PERSON DRILLS ONE-PERSON DRILLS ONE-PERSO
ON DRILLS ONE-PERSON DRILLS ONE-PERSON DRILLS ONE-PERSON DRILLS ONE-PERSON DRILL
S ONE-PERSON DRILLS ONE-PERSON DRILLS ONE-PERSON DRILLS ONE-PI
DRILLS ONE-PERSON DI
ONE-PERSON DRILLS ON

2 Bracing with your left hand and the right (opposite) foot, raise your body off the ground, making sure you remain in balance. Pull the left leg back through the gap formed by your bracing hand and leg.

3 Plant your left foot on the mat where your right hand was. Keep your knees flexed at all times and check your base.

2
Pivoting the legs

This drill not only warms you up, but also develops and improves one of the most essential elements in championship jiu-jitsu: your hip movement. Hips with a lot of swivel and flexibility enable a great guard and guard replacement and are essential for effecting hip escapes. You will use slightly different variations of this movement in many sweeps and escapes from the bottom. Practice the movement both by using the hand to push and by not using it. Both techniques are important to different sweeps.

1 Sit with your arms back and hands on the mat, further apart than shoulder width. It is important that your hands be slightly further apart than they were in the previous drill to allow your legs to swing through. Your legs should be partially extended forward and your feet shoulder-width apart.

2 With your hands on the mat, shift your weight back and to one side slightly (to the left in this case) and raise both feet off the ground an inch or two. While bracing with your left hand, pivot on your buttocks and swing your legs toward the right, bending at the knees until you end up with your right heel touching the right buttock and the sole of your left foot touching the inside of your right thigh. Your weight should slightly rest on your left hand.

3 Pushing off your left hand, with your weight back slightly, pivot off your buttocks and swing your legs toward your left. You may use your feet on the ground slightly to help you circle your legs.

4 You should end up in the opposite position with your weight on your right arm, left heel touching the left buttock and the bottom of the right foot almost touching the inside of your left thigh.

3
Coming up to your knee

This drill is a variation and continuation of drill 2, pivoting the legs. Here Jean Jacques takes it one step further and begins to get up, an important movement used often for a reversal from the guard. Practice the movement forward and backward; it will not only help your reversals and standing-up techniques, but also will tremendously improve your overall balance. Try to feel the balance at all stages of the move.

1 Jean Jacques is sitting down with his legs curled at 90 degrees. His knees are inside his open arms near the elbows.

2 Jean Jacques tucks his left foot in until it is almost touching his right buttocks as he leans forward with his torso. It is very important to have the toes of the left foot pointing forward so they don't interfere with the next movement.

3 Jean Jacques continues to move his upper body forward as he raises his hips off the mat and leans forward with his body. At this point, he is ready to grab a leg or push his opponent back.

4 Jean Jacques finishes the drill by pivoting his left leg back and planting his toes on the mat. From this position he can easily stand up or drive forward.

2 Detail (incorrect) Notice the incorrect way to position the toes. Having the foot pointing forward will make it very difficult for you to move forward with your body because the foot will act as a block.

2 Detail (correct) Notice the correct way to place your foot: the toes are pointing straight and away from the direction of the movement, making it very easy to roll forward.

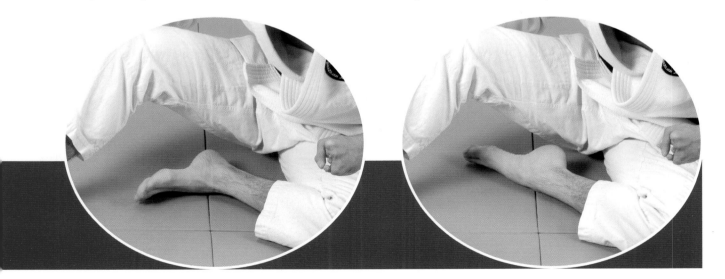

Jumping to your feet

Although this is a difficult drill at first, the move itself is indispensable in jiu-jitsu. As a drill, jumping to your feet develops coordination and explosion; in competition, the move helps counter armlock attacks and facilitates standing up in base to open the closed guard. To be successful, you need to use your arms and learn to coil and uncoil your body for maximum spring off the mat.

1 Kneel on the ground with your hands at your sides. Make sure your buttocks touch your heels and your toes are touching the ground.

ERSON DRILLS ONE-PERSON DRILLS ONE-PERSON DRILLS ONE-PERSON DRILLS ON
DRILLS ONE-PERSON DRILLS ONE-PERSON DRILLS ONE-PERSON DRILLS
ONE-PERSON DRILLS ONE-PERSON DRILLS ONE-PERSON DRILLS ONE-PERSO
ON DRILLS ONE-PERSON DRILLS ONE-PERSON DRILLS ONE-PERSON DRILL
LS ONE-PERSON DRILLS ONE-PERSON DRILLS ONE-PERSON DRILLS ONE-PE
ERSON   ONE-PERSON DRILLS ONE-PERSON DE
DRILLS   SON DRILLS ONE-PERSON DRILLS ON

2 In one movement, using your arms as a pendulum, extend your body and jump up to your feet.

3 Land in base. Make sure to land with your knees bent and as low to the ground as possible.

5
Coming up from the side position

Another very important and useful drill is demonstrated here. This drill increases your hip movement and replicates a movement used often in jiu-jitsu.

1 Lie on your left side on the mat with your legs curled 90 degrees. Your knees should be close to your elbows.

2 Swing your right leg back and use the momentum of the movement, coupled with your left elbow, to raise your torso off the mat.

3 You should end up with you right leg bent and the right foot touching your buttocks while the bottom of the left foot touches the inside of your right thigh. Notice that the final position is the same as the position in drill 2, pivoting the legs. The two can be used in combination as an additional drill.

Getting to your knees from the side position

Jean Jacques demonstrates getting to your knees from the side position—
an extremely useful and effective way to replicate the same movement
used to avoid having your guard passed or to escape from the across-side
position and mount positions (also called the elbow escape). Practicing
and mastering this movement will make your guard defense and escape
much more effective.

1 Lie on the left side of your body with your legs bent and knees close to your elbows. Start the drill by planting your right foot on the mat.

2 Pushing off your right foot and pivoting on your left shoulder, drive your left leg through the gap under your right leg.

3 Start turning your upper body toward the mat. As your left foot gets just past the line of the right one, plant the tip of your left foot on the mat. At this point, you should have both elbows on the mat, and your upper body should be parallel to the mat.

4 Bring you left knee forward until it is parallel to your right one and you are on all fours.

ONE-PERSON DRILLS ONE-PERSON DRILLS ONE-PERSON DRILLS ONE-PERSON
PERSON DRILLS ONE-PERSON DRILLS ONE-PERSON DRILLS ONE-PERSON
DRILLS ONE-PERSON DRILLS ONE-PERSON DRILLS ONE-PERSON
ONE-PERSON DRILLS ONE-PERSON DRILLS ONE-PERSON DRILLS ONE-PERS
SON DRILLS ONE-PERSON DRILLS ONE-PERSON DRILLS ONE-PERSON DRILL
LS ONE-PERSON DRILLS ONE-PERSON DRILLS ONE-PERSON DRILLS ONE-P

7

Circling the legs

Here, John Machado demonstrates the circling-the-legs technique, a drill
that will further loosen your hips and create hip movement. The move is
used often in Brazilian jiu-jitsu, such as when defending a half-guard sweep
or a mount escape counter.

1 Start on all fours with your hands
on the mat, shoulder-width apart,
and your knees slightly further apart.

2 Bracing off your arms, step
out with your left leg . . .

44

PERSON DRILLS ONE-PERSON DRILLS ONE-PERSON DRILLS ONE-PERSON DRILLS ON
DRILLS ONE-PERSON DRILLS ONE-PERSON DRILLS ONE-PERSON DRILLS ONE-PERSON
ONE-PERSON DRILLS ONE-PERSON DRILLS ONE-PERSON DRILLS ONE-PERSO
ON DRILLS ONE-PERSON DRILLS ONE-PERSON DRILLS ONE-PERSON DRILL
LS ONE-PERSON DRILLS ONE-PERSON DRILLS ONE-PERSON DRILLS ONE-PE
ERSON

3 And circle it to your right.

4 Pushing off your arms, lift your torso. Place your weight on the back foot as the left leg passes in front of your body.

5 Continue circling the leg toward your right as your brace off your arms again.

6 Complete the motion by stepping forward with your right foot so that your right knee is up and your hips are facing forward. You should end up in a position that resembles the side control with hips facing the opponent.

ONE-PERSON DRILLS ONE-PERSON DRILLS ONE-PERSON DRILLS ONE-P
PERSON DRILLS ONE-PERSON DRILLS ONE-PERSON DRILLS ONE-PERSON I
RILLS NE-PERSON DRILLS ONE-PERSON DRILLS ONE-PERSON DRILLS ON
ONE-PERSON DRILLS ONE-PERSON DRILLS ONE-PERSON DRILLS ONE-PERS
SON DR LS E-PERSON DRILLS ONE-PERSON DRILLS ONE-PERSON DRILL
LS ON RSO R LLS T RSON DRILLS ONE-PERSON DRILLS ONE-P

8
Side roll

John demonstrates here the side roll, which is used in many escapes and sweeps. Note that the drill's movement is different from the forward roll or breaking a fall because you roll sideways over your shoulder instead of rolling forward.

1 You can start on all fours or with one leg up. John begins here with his left leg up.

2 Brace lightly on the mat with your left hand and tuck your right arm inside your legs as close to the left foot as possible. This will cause your right shoulder to dip toward the mat.

PERSON DRILLS ONE-PERSON DRILLS ONE-PERSON DRILLS ONE-PERSON D
RILLS ONE-PERSON DRILLS ONE-PERSON DRILLS ONE-PERSON DRILLS ON
NE-PERSON DRILLS ONE-PERSON DRILLS ONE-PERSON DRILLS ONE-PERSO
N DRILLS ONE-PERSON DRILLS ONE-PERSON DRILLS ONE-PERSON DRILLS
S ONE-PERSON DRILLS ONE-PERSON DRILLS ONE-PERSON DRILLS ONE-PE
RSO   ONE-PERSON DRILLS ONE-PERSON DR
DRILL   ONE-PERSON

3 Place the right side of your head on the mat and push off your left leg to start to roll over your shoulder toward the right.

4 Continue rolling over your shoulder, and turn your legs from left to right in a circular motion as they pass over your head.

5 Your left knee should touch the mat on the opposite side, and you should finish the position in a stance similar to the one you started in. You can continuously do these rolls back and forward.

9
Wrestler's drill

The wrestler's drill simulates going to the back, changing hips in side control, or escaping from back control in the all-fours position. It develops both your hip and your ground movement and has a variety of other applications.

1 John starts off on all fours with his knees slightly more than shoulder-width apart and the elbows close to the knees. Notice that John's toes are cocked and ready to push off the mat, springing him into action. He does not have his feet straight, which would slow him down and add one more step to the movement, costing him precious fractions of a second.

2 John steps off with his left leg and plants his foot out. His left knee points up, and his left arm is no longer touching the mat.

3 Bracing off his left foot and right arm, John shoots his right leg out between the gap formed by his left foot and right arm. Notice that John's hips are facing forward and his left foot is firmly planted on the mat. At this point, John has his weight resting on four points: his right forearm, his right buttock, the left foot, and the outside of his right foot. However, he maintains his body's readiness to move by keeping his right forearm and left foot bracing.

4 John throws his left leg forward in a circular motion toward his right until his foot lands in line with his right forearm. Notice that John used his right toes to help the move.

5 John ends up in the same position he started in, but faces the opposite direction. Repeat the drill going back and forth or in a continuous circular motion.

10

Hip escape

Most practitioners have learned the standard hip escape drill and practice it regularly. Here, however, Jean Jacques demonstrates a modified elbow escape (one of the primary techniques used to escape from the mounted position) that ensures the ability to escape even the toughest mount and be able to replace the guard. What he introduces here is the concept of making a frame with the arms. The frame has two purposes: 1) you give yourself a target for your knee to come in, helping you focus for the real hip escape/guard replacement, and 2) you use the frame to block the opponent's hip as you escape the hip. Contrary to the old standard elbow escape (where you would push the knee out with your elbow or hands), this technique blocks the opponent's hips and knee with the frame, making it a more powerful move.

1 Jean Jacques starts lying on his side with his right leg bent and right foot firmly planted on the mat. His left elbow touches the mat, and his forearm is straight up, forming the bottom part of the frame. His right arm is bent at 90 degrees and forms the top part of the frame. His left hand pushes on the back of his right hand, giving it support. The left leg can be straight and lying on the ground or slightly curled up, as he starts the motion here.

2 Pushing off his right leg, Jean Jacques slides his hips to his right, jackknifing his body while holding the frame stationary. He visualizes the frame blocking the opponent's hips with his right forearm and the opponent's right knee with his left elbow.

3 Still pushing off his right foot, Jean Jacques slides his hips back to his left and drives his left knee inside the frame (or target) that he created with his arms. That would be exactly the inside of the opponent's hips, the perfect place for the guard replacement/elbow escape from the mounted position.

4 Jean Jacques pushes off his left leg and right foot and goes back to center, a neutral position that simulates being mounted.

Pulling your body down

Although this drill looks similar to drill 10, the hip escape, it has the opposite effect. In the hip escape, you place one foot on the mat and push off it as you coil your body while you move your hip out. In this case, you are actually trying to pull your body down with your heels. This is very useful in many half-guard positions where you need to get your head and torso closer to the opponent's center.

1 Have your back on the mat, both legs curled, and both feet planted on the mat close to your buttocks.

2 Kick both legs out and to your right as far as possible, as you roll to your right side. Use the explosive motion to drive your body in the direction of the kick.

PERSON DRILLS ONE-PERSON DRILLS ONE-PERSON DRILLS ONE-PERSON DRILLS ON
RILLS ONE-PERSON DRILLS ONE-PERSON DRILLS ONE-PERSON DRILLS
NE-PERSON DRILLS ONE-PERSON DRILLS ONE-PERSON DRILLS ONE-PERSO
ON DRILLS ONE-PERSON DRILLS ONE-PERSON DRILLS ONE-PERSON DRILLS
LS ONE-PERSON DRILLS ONE-PERSON DRILLS ONE-PERSON DRILLS ONE-PE
ERSON DE
RILLS ON

3 Plant both heels on the mat as far out and as far to the right as you can. Your body should be sideways.

4 Pulling off your heel and pivoting on your right shoulder, drive your body toward your feet, coiling it. Bring your right knee up and your right elbow down toward each other.

ONE-PERSON DRILLS ONE-PERSON DRILLS ONE-PERSON DRILLS ONE-PERSON DRILL
PERSON DRILLS ONE-PERSON DRILLS ONE-PERSON DRILLS ONE-P
DRILLS ONE-PERSON DRILLS ONE-PERSON DRILLS ONE-PERSON DR
ONE-PERSON DRILLS ONE-PERSON DRILLS ONE-PERSON DRILLS ONE-PERS
SON DRILLS ONE-PERSON DRILLS ONE-PERSON DRILLS ONE-PERSON DRIL
LS ONE-PERSON DRILLS ONE-PERSON DRILLS ONE-PERSON DRILLS ONE-P

12
Push-up, spring to feet

This is a fabulous drill for Brazilian jiu-jitsu practitioners. It not only increases agility, but it also has many applications in various positions. For example, you'd use a motion similar to springing to your feet to apply an armlock from the side. The same or similar motion is used to achieve the knee-on-the-stomach position.

1 Jean Jacques lies flat on the mat with face down. He has both arms cocked and his hands planted on the ground at mid-chest level. His toes are pressing against the mat.

2 Jean Jacques pushes up off his arms in a motion similar to a push-up, except that he doesn't bring his entire body off the mat but rather rocks off his knees.

ON DRILLS ONE-PERSON DRILLS ONE-PERSON DRILLS ONE-PERSON DRILLS ON
ONE-PERSON DRILLS ONE-PERSON DRILLS ONE-PERSON DRILLS ONE-PERSO
ON DRILLS ONE-PERSON DRILLS ONE-PERSON DRILLS ONE-PERSON DRILLS
S ONE-PERSON DRILLS ONE-PERSON DRILLS ONE-PERSON DRILLS ONE-PI
RSON DRILLS ONE-PERSON DRILLS ONE-PERSON DRILLS ONE-PERSON DR
RILLS ONE-PERSON DRILLS ONE-PERSON DRILLS ONE-PERSON DRILLS ON

3 In one jump, pushing off his toes and arms, Jean Jacques brings his legs forward and under him, landing with one foot under his body and the other one back slightly.

TWO-PERSON DRILLS

Timing is very important in most sports, but it is essential in Brazilian jiu-jitsu. When you are a beginner fighting against another beginner, you may have the luxury to execute moves slowly because your opponent is also slow to recognize threats and react. As you progress in belt and rank, however, the ability to execute a technique quickly and correctly frequently means the difference between success and failure—especially at the highest levels, where you may see an opening for a technique but your body may not be fast enough to react with the proper technique in a precise manner. These two-person drills simulate moves you will use when you train and compete and present a good route for making fast progress.

As mentioned, it is extremely important when executing drills that you concentrate on precision and technique rather than speed. Repeat each drill 10 times per side with a willing partner. Using a variety of partners will help you get used to different body types and weights. Of course, you should alternate who is doing the reps between each set. To keep things interesting, add your own variations and make your partner give you more resistance or less resistance as you master the drill.

ON DRILLS TWO-PERSON DRILLS TWO-PERSON DRILLS TWO-PERSON DRILL
LLS TWO-PERSON DRILLS TWO-PERSON DRILLS TWO-PERSON DRILLS TWO
TWO-PERSON DRILLS TWO-PERSON DRILLS TWO-PERSON DRILLS TWO-PER
PERSON DRILLS TWO-PERSON DRILLS TWO-PERSON DRILLS TWO-PERSON
ON DRILLS TWO-PERSON DRILLS TWO-PERSON DRILLS TWO-PERSON DRIL
RILLS TWO-PERSON DRILLS TWO-PERSON DRILLS TWO-PERSON DRILLS TW

13

Replacing the guard

This extremely important and fun drill will improve your game tremendously by developing your overall body coordination and your abilities to
roll over your shoulders and to use your feet and legs to replace the guard.
The drill mimics replacing the guard when your opponent is standing up just
after passing. It is critical to remain in contact and control of your partner
when practicing this drill because you must practice the way you will spar
and compete. If you don't control your opponent in competition, he will
simply follow your move around and end up on side control.

1 Jean Jacques is lying on the mat with his legs
curled, the soles of his feet touching the mat,
and his arms bent with elbows touching his torso.
His partner, Todd, stands up behind him.

2 Pushing off his feet, Jean Jacques throws
his legs over his head, bending at the
waist as he rolls backward, and reaching with
his hands inside Todd's legs.

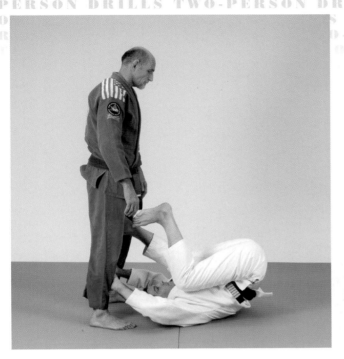

3 Jean Jacques grabs the inside of Todd's calves and helps pull himself back over until his left leg touches the inside of Todd's left calf.

4 Pushing off his left leg and arm, Jean Jacques opens his legs and spins his torso toward the right. It is critical for Jean Jacques to remain in contact with Todd at all times, so he uses his hands and foot to control Todd, keeping him from either walking away or following him as he spins around.

5 As he starts to face Todd, Jean Jacques switches his left leg from touching Todd's left leg to hooking his right one and then releases the left-hand grip on Todd's calf. Again it is very important to remain in contact and control of the opponent at all times; otherwise, he will follow your movement and come across-side.

DRILLS TWO-PERSON DRILLS TWO-PERSON DRILLS TWO-PERSON DRILL
LS TWO-PERSON DRILLS TWO-PERSON DRILLS TWO-PERSON DRILLS TWO
WO-PERSON DRILLS TWO-PERSON DRILLS TWO-PERSON DRILLS TWO-PER
PERSON DRILLS TWO-PERSON DRILLS TWO-PERSON DRILLS TWO-PERSON
ON DRILLS TWO-PERSON DRILLS TWO-PERSON DRILLS TWO-PERSON DRILL
RILLS TWO-PERSON DRILLS TWO-PERSON DRILLS TWO-PERSON DRILLS TW

14

Armlock 1

Jean Jacques demonstrates a drill for the armlock from the side.

1 Jean Jacques is on his knees on John's left side with his arms locked around John's left arm. Jean Jacques's left arm is hooked under John's arm, and his left hand is locked onto his right wrist. His right hand grips John's left wrist.

2 Jean Jacques takes a big step forward with his right leg, passing his foot over John's head and planting it in front of John's face. Notice that Jean Jacques has raised his hips to help the move.

TWO-PERSON DRILLS TWO-PERSON DRILLS TWO-PERSON DRILLS TWO-PERSON I
ERSON DRILLS TWO-PERSON DRILLS TWO-PERSON DRILLS TWO-PERSON I
DRILLS TWO-PERSON DRILLS TWO-PERSON DRILLS TWO-PERSON DRILLS
LS TWO-PERSON DRILLS TWO-PERSON DRILLS TWO-PERSON DRILLS TWO
TWO-PERSON DRILLS TWO-PERSON DRILLS TWO-PERSON DRILLS TWO-PER
ERSON DRILLS TWO-PERSON DRILLS TWO-PERSON DRILLS TWO-PERSON I
ON DRILLS TWO-PERSON DRILLS TWO-PERSON DRILLS TWO-PERSON DRILL

3 Jean Jacques falls back for the armlock. Notice the perfect form as his right foot is planted right in front of John's face and his knees are closed, removing any space that John could exploit to remove his elbow. Jean Jacques's right leg keeps John from defending the armlock by rolling over to his left on top of Jean Jacques. Jean Jacques's left shin, pushing against John's left side, keeps John from spinning to his left.

15

Armlock 2: surfing drill

Jean Jacques here demonstrates the surfing drill that simulates the armlock from the side. This is a two-man drill that when mastered will yield split-second armlocks.

1 Jean Jacques lies on top of John in a side-control position. Both of John's arms are curled under Jean Jacques. Jean Jacques has both of his arms on John's right side.

2 Initiating the drill, John pushes Jean Jacques up with both arms. Jean Jacques plants his hands on the mat, shifting a small amount of his weight onto his own hands, but the majority of his weight should be carried by John's arms. At the same time, Jean Jacques extends his legs slightly, driving his hips forward so they move near John's left arm.

WO-PERSON DRILLS TWO-PERSON DRILLS TWO-PERSON DRILLS TWO-PERSON I
DRILLS TWO-PERSON DRILLS TWO-PERSON DRILLS TWO-PERSON DRILLS
LS TWO-PERSON DRILLS TWO-PERSON DRILLS TWO-PERSON DRILLS TWO
TWO-PERSON DRILLS TWO-PERSON DRILLS TWO-PERSON DRILLS TWO-PER
ERSON DRILLS -PERSON I
N DRILLS SON DRILL
TWO

3 Using the move shown in Drill 12, Jean Jacques pushes with his arms and springs to his feet with his right foot over John's head and his left shin touching John's left ribcage.

4 Jean Jacques quickly falls back for the armlock. The secret here is that Jean Jacques drops his hips straight down next to John's side so John won't be able to pull his elbow out. At the same time, Jean Jacques's arms wrap John's left arm before he drops his torso to the mat.

DRILLS TWO-PERSON DRILLS TWO-PERSON DRILLS TWO-PERSON DRILLS TWO-PERSON DRILL
LS TWO-PERSON DRILLS TWO-PERSON DRILLS TWO-PERSON DRILLS TWO
PERSON DRILLS TWO-PERSON DRILLS TWO-PERSON DRILLS TWO-PER
PERSON DRILLS TWO-PERSON DRILLS TWO-PERSON DRILLS TWO-PERSON
ON DRILLS TWO-PERSON DRILLS TWO-PERSON DRILLS TWO-PERSON DRILL
RILLS TWO-PERSON DRILLS TWO-PERSON DRILLS TWO-PERSON DRILLS TW

16

Knee-on-stomach 1: hopping from side to side

The ability to change sides and maintain the knee-on-stomach position cannot be overemphasized. The knee-on-stomach is a very dynamic controlling position; as opponents move and turn, you must be able to move with them and retain the control. Here Jean Jacques shows a great drill that will not only help you maintain the position but also increase your agility.

1 Jean Jacques starts on John's left side with his left knee on John's stomach. His right leg is opened with his foot planted on the mat and the knee up. His left foot is hooked on John's left ribcage. Jean Jacques puts both hands on John's upper body.

2 John begins the drill by turning to his left. Jean Jacques places both hands on John's right arm . . .

3 And puts his weight on his hands to keep John pinned and to help assist his movement as he hops over John's body with his left leg.

TWO-PERSON DRILLS TWO-PERSON DRILLS TWO-PERSON DRILLS TWO-PERSON
N DRILLS TWO-PERSON DRILLS TWO-PERSON DRILLS TWO-PERSON DRILL
LS TWO-PERSON DRILLS TWO-PERSON DRILLS TWO-PERSON DRILLS TWO
TWO-PERSON DRILLS TWO-PERSON DRILLS TWO-PERSON DRILLS TWO-PER
PERSON DRILLS TWO-PERSON DRILLS TWO-PERSON DRILLS TWO-PERSON
ON DRILLS TWO-PERSON DRILLS

4 Jean Jacques lands on John's right side, still pressing against the shoulders with his arms, cocks his right leg . . .

5 And puts the right knee on John's right ribcage.

6 As John turns to his right, Jean Jacques releases the pressure on John's arm, allowing him to spin. Jean Jacques replaces the hand pressure on the opposite shoulder. To repeat the drill, Jean Jacques would now hop over to the left.

DRILLS TWO-PERSON DRILLS TWO-PERSON DRILLS TWO-PERSON DRILL
LS TWO-PERSON DRILLS TWO-PERSON DRILLS TWO-PERSON DRILLS TWO
WO-PERSON DRILLS TWO-PERSON DRILLS TWO-PERSON DRILLS TWO
PERSON DRILLS TWO-PERSON DRILLS TWO-PERSON DRILLS TWO-PER
DRILLS TWO-PERSON DRILLS TWO-PERSON DRILLS TWO-PERSON
DRILLS TWO-PERSON DRILLS TWO-PERSON DRILLS TWO-PERSON
RILLS TWO-PERSON DRILLS TWO-PERSON DRILLS TWO-PERSON DRILL

17

Knee-on-stomach 2: walking around

In this drill, Jean Jacques maintains contact with John at all times while he walks around his opponent rather than hopping over. Because this move allows greater control of your opponent, it may be more effective in the event of a large adversary or when your opponent moves more slowly and deliberately.

1 Jean Jacques starts the drill on John's left side with his left knee on John's stomach and his left hand pushing on John's chest.

2 John turns to his left, into Jean Jacques. Jean Jacques pushes off his left arm, controlling John's turning speed.

3 Jean Jacques steps off to his right with his right leg and releases his left knee-on-stomach, planting his left foot next to John's left side as he maintains the pressure against John's chest with his left arm.

4 Jean Jacques continues stepping around John's head. He walks around to his right and prepares to change sides as he reaches with his right hand toward John's right side.

TWO-PERSON DRILLS TWO-PERSON DRILLS TWO-PERSON DRILLS TWO-PERSON D
DRILLS TWO-PERSON DRILLS TWO-PERSON DRILLS TWO-PERSON DRILLS
LS TWO-PERSON DRILLS TWO-PERSON DRILLS TWO-PERSON DRILLS TWO
TWO-PERSON DRILLS TWO-PERSON DRILLS TWO-PERSON DRILLS TWO-PERS
ERSON DRILLS TWO-PERSON DRILLS TWO-PERSON DRILLS TWO-PERSON D
N DRILLS TWO-PERSON DRILLS TWO-PERSON DRILLS TWO-PERSON DRILL
TWO

5 Jean Jacques continues walking around John's head to his right and plants his right hand on John's chest.

6 John continues the drill by turning to his right. Jean Jacques places his right knee on John's stomach . . .

7 And pushes John's chest down with his right arm, as he drops his weight forward.

8 John turns to his right, and Jean Jacques repeats the motion, going around John's head to his left.

ON DRILLS TWO-PERSON DRILLS TWO-PERSON DRILLS TWO-PERSON DRILLS TWO-PERSON DRIL
LLS TWO-PERSON DRILLS TWO-PERSON DRILLS TWO-PERSON DRILLS TWO
TWO-PERSON DRILLS TWO-PERSON DRILLS TWO-PERSON DRILLS TWO-PER
PERSON DRILLS TWO-PERSON DRILLS TWO-PERSON DRILLS TWO-PERSON
ON DRILLS TWO-PERSON DRILLS TWO-PERSON DRILLS TWO-PERSON DRIL
RILLS TWO-PERSON DRILLS TWO-PERSON DRILLS TWO-PERSON DRILLS TW
TWO-PERSON DRILLS TWO-PERSON DRILLS TWO

18

Hip escape: guard replace and sweep

This is one of the most complete two-person drills, as it not only uses the hip escape, which applies to both replacing the guard and to escaping the mounted position, but it also simulates replacing the guard and going on to a reversal.

1 The drill begins with John across-side on Jean Jacques, with his right arm around Jean Jacques's head and his left arm hugging Jean Jacques's right arm.

1 Reverse Angle We reverse the angle for better viewing. Jean Jacques puts his right foot on the mat and coils his left leg with his knee up, pressing against John's left side to keep him from mounting.

2 Jean Jacques steps out with his right leg as he escapes his hips to his right and turns his body to his left.

3 Jean Jacques brings his left leg in and slides his left knee in, placing his left shin in front of John's hips.

4 Jean Jacques grabs John's left sleeve at the elbow with his right hand and steps slightly to his left with his right foot as he turns his body into John. With his left hand, Jean Jacques grabs John's right gi pants near the knee.

5 Jean Jacques quickly turns his body to his right. Since John's weight rests on Jean Jacques's left shin, it becomes easy to sweep him over as he pulls the right sleeve in and lifts the left leg up.

N DRILLS TWO-PERSON DRILLS TWO-PERSON DRILLS TWO-PERSON DRILL
LLS TWO-PERSON DRILLS TWO-PERSON DRILLS TWO-PERSON DRILLS TWO
TWO-PERSON DRILLS TWO-PERSON DRILLS TWO-PERSON DRILLS TWO-PER
PERSON DRILLS TWO-PERSON DRILLS TWO-PERSON DRILLS TWO-PERSON I
ON DRILLS TWO-PERSON DRILLS TWO-PERSON DRILLS TWO-PERSON DRIL
RILLS TWO-PERSON DRILLS TWO-PERSON DRILLS TWO-PERSON DRILLS TW

6 Jean Jacques ends up on top of John, still holding the gi pants and maintaining the knee-on-stomach.

7 Jean Jacques drops down to the starting position.

TWO-PERSON DRILLS TWO-PERSON DRILLS TWO-PERSON DRILLS TWO-PER
PERSON DRILLS TWO-PERSON DRILLS TWO-PERSON DRILLS TWO-PERSON
DRILLS TWO-PERSON DRILLS TWO-PERSON DRILLS TWO-PERSON DRILLS
LS TWO-PERSON DRILLS TWO-PERSON DRILLS TWO-PERSON DRILLS TWO
TWO-PERSON DRILLS TWO-PERSON DRILLS TWO-PERSON DRILLS TWO-PER
PERSON DRILLS TWO-PERSON DRILLS TWO-PERSON DRILLS TWO-PERSON

8 John now executes the same drill, ending up in the start position.

19

Escape from side control

This drill also facilitates escaping from the across-side position.
It replicates the hip escape and turning to your knees.

1 John begins the drill in side control, but this time his right arm is over Jean Jacques's head with his elbow close to his ear, and his left hand is blocking Jean Jacques's left hip, preventing him from sliding his knee in.

2 Jean Jacques brings his left knee in to keep John from mounting.

3 He plants his right foot out and escapes his hips to his right.

WO-PERSON DRILLS TWO-PERSON DRILLS TWO-PERSON DRILLS TWO-PER
ERSON DRILLS TWO-PERSON DRILLS TWO-PERSON DRILLS TWO-PERSON D
DRILLS TWO-PERSON DRILLS TWO-PERSON DRILLS TWO-PERSON DRILLS
LS TWO-PERSON DRILLS TWO-PERSON DRILLS TWO-PERSON DRILLS TWO
WO-PERSON DRILLS TWO-PERSON DRILLS TWO-PERSON DRILLS TWO-PERS
ERSON   O-PERSON DRILLS TWO-PERSON D
ON D   RSON DRILLS TWO-PERSON DRILL
                                         PERSON DRILLS TWO

4 Jean Jacques slides his left leg under his right leg as he turns to his stomach.

5 Jean Jacques slides his right arm inside John's arm and reaches around John's left leg as he continues turning to his stomach. Notice that Jean Jacques is pushing off his right foot with the toes firmly pressing against the mat and is maintaining pressure on the right shoulder to prevent John from coming forward and flattening him back to the mat.

6 Once he has turned completely to his stomach, Jean Jacques pushes off his toes and grabs John's left thigh.

7 Jean Jacques pulls himself in and completes the escape. Notice that this is the same motion as Drill 6.

7 Different Angle Jean Jacques ends up on his knees, grabbing John's left leg, and with John's chest on his back.

74

8 Jean Jacques steps out with his right leg . . .

9 Shoots his left leg through as in drill 9, the wrestler's drill . . .

10 And comes back to the start position.

FIGHTING TECHNIQUES

These fighting techniques were selected by Jean Jacques and John to give you a complete and competitive game of escapes, reversals, and attacks. The techniques are designed to expand your circle of moves and complement the ones presented in *Black Belt Techniques.* The movements presented here will give you powerful options to achieve success in almost any combat situation.

FIGHTING TECHNIQUES FIGHTING TECHNIQUES FIGHTING TECHNIQUES FIGHTING TECHNIQUES FIGHTING TECHNIQUES FIGHTING TECHNIQUES FIGHTING TECHNIQUE FIGHTING TECHNIQUES FIGHTING TECHNIQUES FIGHTING TECHNIQUES FIGHTING TECHNIQUES FIGHTING TECHNIQUES FIGHTING TE FIGHTING TECHNIQUES FIGHTING TECHNIQUES FIGHTING TECHNIQUES FIGHTING TECHNIQUES FIGHTING TECHNIQUES FIG FIGHTING TECHNIQUES FIGHTING TECHNIQUES FIGHTING TECHNIQUES FIGHTING TECHNI FIGHTING TECHNIQUES FIGHTING TECHNIQUES FIGHTING TECHNIQUES FIGHTING

20

Half-guard sweep 1

Traditionally, the half-guard was regarded as a defensive position, a transition between having the guard passed and replacing the guard. Today's fighters, however, have developed many sweeps, reversals, and even submissions from the half-guard. In this technique, Jean Jacques uses a movement very similar to drill 10, the hip escape, to place his knee inside the opponent and, after dominating the elbow, sweep the opponent toward the blocked elbow. The key to this move is blocking the elbow on the same side that your top leg comes in. After you escape the hip and create the space to slide your knee in, your opponent will generally try to place his weight on your top leg to keep tight. The shin will prevent him from coming too close to you and actually help the sweep, as his weight is off the ground and resting on your shin.

1 Jean Jacques has John in his half-guard, the result of a variety of circumstances. John may have been passing the guard, or Jean Jacques may have been escaping from the mounted position or may have pulled half-guard, looking for a sweep. Jean Jacques traps John's right leg with his right shin and slides his hips to his left (see drill 10, the hip escape) while at the same time controlling John's right arm with both of his own arms. It is extremely important to keep control over John's right shin; otherwise, he will just move over to side control.

1 Reverse Angle Jean Jacques creates the space by bracing his arms against John. His left arm pushes against John's chest, and his right arm secures John's left sleeve right at the wrist, keeping him from using his left arm to hold on to Jean Jacques's head.

FIGHTING TECHNIQUES FIGHTING TECHNIQUES FIGHTING TECHNIQUES FIGHTING TECHN
NIQUES FIGHTING TECHNIQUES FIGHTING TECHNIQUES FIGHTING TECHNIQUES FIGHTIN
ING TECHNIQUES FIGHTING TECHNIQUES FIGHTING TECHNIQUES FIGHTIN
ES FIGHTING TECHNIQUES FIGHTING TECHNIQUES FIGHTING TECHNIQUES
TECHNIQUES FIGHTING TECHNIQUES FIGHTING TECHNIQUES FIGHTING TI
GHTIN FIGHTING TECHNIQUES FIGH
IQUES CHNIQUES FIGHTING TECHNI

2 Jean Jacques then drives his torso in, pushing John's left arm back, and slides his right arm under John's left leg until he grabs John's wrist.

2 Reverse Angle

3 At this point, Jean Jacques has control over John's left arm with his own right arm under the left leg. While using his right leg to trap John's right leg, Jean Jacques slides his left knee in front of John's right shoulder in the space created by his escape.

TING TECHNIQUES FIGHTING TECHNIQUES FIGHTING TECHNIQUES FIGHTI
JES FIGHTING TECHNIQUES FIGHTING TECHNIQUES FIGHTING TECHNIQUE
TECHNIQUES FIGHTING TECHNIQUES FIGHTING TECHNIQUES FIGHTING TE
FIGHTING TECHNIQUES FIGHTING TECHNIQUES FIGHTING TECHNIQUES FI
NIQUES FIGHTING TECHNIQUES FIGHTING TECHNIQUES FIGHTING TECHNI
NG TECHNIQUES FIGHTING TECHNIQUES FIGHTING TECHNIQUES FIGHTIN

4 He then grabs John's right wrist with his left hand, preventing John from bracing to his right as he is being swept, and opens his left leg out, placing his left shin in front of John's right biceps or elbow.

5 In one movement, Jean Jacques pushes off his right foot, pulls up on his right arm to lift John's left leg, pulls John's right sleeve, and opens his left leg out—initiating the sweep to his left. John cannot block the sweep because his right arm is held by Jean Jacques's left hand and his arm and right leg are still trapped by Jean Jacques's right heel.

NIQUES FIGHTING TECHNIQUES FIGHTING TECHNIQUES FIGHTING TECHNI
ING TECHNIQUES FIGHTING TECHNIQUES FIGHTING TECHNIQUES FIGHTIN
ES FIGHTING TECHNIQUES FIGHTING TECHNIQUES FIGHTING TECHNIQUES
TECHNIQUES FIGHTING TECHNIQUES FIGHTING TECHNIQUES FIGHTING TI
GHTING TECHNIQUES FIGHTING TECHNIQUES FIGHTING TECHNIQUES FIGH
IQUES   CHNIQUES FIGHTING TECHNIC

6 As they roll to the left, Jean Jacques braces his left arm on the mat and pushes off it to get on top of John. Notice that Jean Jacques maintains the grip on John's left arm under the leg, thereby hindering John's ability to initiate a hip escape by placing his foot on the mat.

7 Jean Jacques completes the reversal by wrapping his left arm under John's head and grabbing the gi as he drives his chest on John's chest for tightness—achieving the 2 points for the reversal!

TING TECHNIQUES FIGHTING TECHNIQUES FIGHTING TECHNIQUES FIGHTI
UES FIGHTING TECHNIQUES FIGHTING TECHNIQUES FIGHTING TECHNIQUES FIGHTI
TECHNIQUES FIGHTING TECHNIQUES FIGHTING TECHNIQUES FIGHTING TECHNIQUE
FIGHTING TECHNIQUES FIGHTING TECHNIQUES FIGHTING TECHNIQUES FIGHTING TE
NIQUES FIGHTING TECHNIQUES FIGHTING TECHNIQUES FIGHTING TECHNIQUES FI
NG TECHNIQUES FIGHTING TECHNIQUES FIGHTING TECHNIQUES FIGHTING TECHNI
ING TECHNIQUES FIGHTING TECHNIQUES FIGHTING TECHNIQUES FIGHTING TECHNIN

21

Half-guard sweep 2

In the previous technique Jean Jacques was able to prevent John's arm from controlling his head or sliding under the armpit (both very effective controls). This time, however, Jean Jacques was late and John achieved great control with his left arm inside Jean Jacques's right arm under the armpit. This is a classic half-guard position, and if Jean Jacques doesn't react properly, John will pass his guard, gaining 3 points. However, here Jean Jacques uses a motion similar to drill 10, the hip escape, to slide his knee inside John's hips and execute the reversal for a 2-point gain of his own.

1 Jean Jacques is on the bottom and has John in his half-guard. He has trapped John's left leg with his own left leg, locking his left foot into a figure-four under his right leg at the knee. John's left arm is inside Jean Jacques's right arm under the armpit, giving him solid control. Jean Jacques holds John's gi with his right hand.

2 Jean Jacques opens his right leg out, plants his right foot on the mat, and uses it to push his hips to his right.

3 Jean Jacques circles his right arm in front of John's chest, pushes on it to create distance, and slides his right knee in front of John's hips. Notice again that Jean Jacques uses his left leg to trap John's left leg throughout the move. Otherwise, John will move to his side for the guard pass.

4 Jean Jacques drives his right leg forward, pushing John back slightly and creating space for his right arm to continue to circle and slide under John's left arm. At this point, John normally tries to push his body, especially his hips, forward onto Jean Jacques to take away the space Jean Jacques has just created.

5 Using John's pressure against him, Jean Jacques quickly opens his right leg out wide, releasing the right knee from John's hips as he shoots his right arm up. John cannot help but to fall forward.

6 Jean Jacques sits up and grabs John's right leg with both hands.

7 Driving his chest onto John's left side and pulling on the right leg forces John to fall to his right. As he starts to get on top, Jean Jacques throws his right leg over, which brings him fully on top and completes the sweep for 2 points.

6 Reverse Angle Notice how Jean Jacques grabs John's right knee with his left hand and his right ankle with his right hand, preventing John from opening the leg up to block the sweep. At the same time, Jean Jacques drives his head and chest onto John's left hip, forcing him to fall to his right.

TING TECHNIQUES FIGHTING TECHNIQUES FIGHTING TECHNIQUES FIGHTI
UES FIGHTING TECHNIQUES FIGHTING TECHNIQUES FIGHTING TECHNIQUE
TECHNI   FIGHTING TECHNIQUES FIGHTING TECHNIQUES FIGHTING TE
FIGHTING   IQUES FIGHTING TECHNIQUES FIGHTING TECHNIQUES FI
NIQUES   IQUES FIGHTING TECHNIQUES FIGHTING TECHNI
ING TECHNIQUES FIGHTING TECHNIQUES FIGHTING TECHNIQUES FIGHTIN

22

Half-guard sweep 3

In the previous position, Jean Jacques reacted early and blocked John's arm from reaching his lapel or sliding under the armpit for control. In this situation, however, Jean Jacques was slightly late, and John was able to slip his left arm under Jean Jacques's right armpit, gaining control and an advantageous position. If Jean Jacques doesn't react properly at this point, John will pass the guard using the cross-knee technique and score 3 points. Instead, Jean Jacques makes clever use of John's lapel for the sweep.

1 John is on top in Jean Jacques's half-guard and has achieved good control with his left arm inside Jean Jacques's right arm near the armpit. With his right hand, Jean Jacques quickly opens John's left lapel. Notice that Jean Jacques has trapped John's leg by applying a figure-four with his legs to make it more difficult for John to pass the guard.

2 Jean Jacques opens his right leg out, plants his foot on the mat, and uses it to slide his hips out toward his right to create space between himself and John. With his left arm, Jean Jacques holds John's right arm at the elbow to prevent him from bracing to block the sweep to his right.

3 Jean Jacques then hooks his right foot just inside of John's left leg. Notice that Jean Jacques keeps his left shin on top of John's left leg at all times to deny him the freedom of coming around for the pass.

4 Jean Jacques pulls up on his right arm, which controls John's lapel, forcing his body toward his head. At the same time, Jean Jacques uses his right foot hook to lift John's legs . . .

5 And continues the rotation to his left until he has reversed the position for 2 points.

FIGHTING TECHNIQUES FIGHTING TECHNIQUES FIGHTING TECHNIQUES FIGHTING TECH
TING TECHNIQUES FIGHTING TECHNIQUES FIGHTING TECHNIQUES FIGHTING TECHNIQUES FIGHTI
UES FIGHTING TECHNIQUES FIGHTING TECHNIQUES FIGHTING TECHNIQUE
TECHNIQUES FIGHTING TECHNIQUES FIGHTING TECHNIQUES FIGHTING TE
FIGHTING TECHNIQUES FIGHTING TECHNIQUES FIGHTING TECHNIQUES FI
NIQUES FIGHTING TECHNIQUES FIGHTING TECHNIQUES FIGHTING TECHNI
ING TECHNIQUES FIGHTING TECHNIQUES FIGHTING TECHNIQUES FIGHTIN

23

Half-guard sweep 3 (variation)

In this sequence from the previous position, Jean Jacques begins to sweep as in step 22.3, but John reacts quickly and opens his right leg, bracing out and blocking the sweep. Jean Jacques quickly adjusts and goes for a second sweep option. This is the essence of Jean Jacques's game. As he states, you work with small circles; you pull here and lift there, and if your opponent falls, great. If he doesn't, you need to have other options instantly at hand and pull there and lift here until he goes. We pick up the position from the point at which Jean Jacques already has his hook in and begins to sweep (22.3).

1 Jean Jacques has achieved the position he needs to sweep. His right foot is hooked under John's left leg, his left shin traps John's left shin, his right hand controls the lapel, and his left arm holds John's right arm at the elbow to prevent him from extending it to block the sweep.

2 As Jean Jacques begins to sweep to John's right, John quickly opens his right leg to block the move.

FIGHTING TECHNIQUES FIGHTING TECHNIQUES FIGHTING TECHNIQUES FIGHTING TECHNIQUES FIGHTING TECHNI NIQUES FIGHTING TECHNIQUES FIGHTING TECHNIQUES FIGHTING TECHNIQUES FIGHTING TECHNI ING TECHNIQUES FIGHTING TECHNIQUES FIGHTING TECHNIQUES FIGHTING TECHNIQUES FIGHTIN ES FIGHTING TECHNIQUES FIGHTING TECHNIQUES FIGHTING TECHNIQUES FIGHTING TECHNIQUES TECHNIQUES FIGHTING TECHNIQUES FIGHTING TECHNIQUES FIGHTING TECHNIQUES FIGHTING TE GHTING TECHNIQUES FIGHTING TECHNIQUES FIGHTING TECHNIQUES FIGHTING TECHNIQUES FIGH IQUES FIGHTING TECHNIQUES FIGHTING TECHNIQUES FIGHTING TECHNIQUES FIGHTING TECHNIQ

3 Jean Jacques then wraps his left arm under John's right knee and slides his body in under John.

4 Pushing off his left leg, Jean Jacques turns his body toward his own right. He pulls down on John's lapel with his right arm, eases the pressure on his right hook to lower John's leg, and drives his left arm, with John's right leg, over to his right.

5 Jean Jacques continues to roll to his right, sweeping John to that side. Notice that Jean Jacques continues to hold on to John's lapel and leg throughout this movement.

6 As soon as the sweep is complete and he has John's back flat on the ground, Jean Jacques releases his right foot hook and places that leg flat on the mat, ending up across-side.

FIGHTING TECHNIQUES FIGHTING TECHNIQUES FIGHTING TECHN
TING TECHNIQUES FIGHTING TECHNIQUES FIGHTING TECHNIQUES FIGHTI
UES FIGHTING TECHNIQUES FIGHTING TECHNIQUES FIGHTING TECHNIQUE
TECHNIQUES FIGHTING TECHNIQUES FIGHTING TECHNIQUES FIGHTING TE
FIGHTING TECHNIQUES FIGHTING TECHNIQUES FIGHTING TECHNIQUES FI
NIQUES FIGHTING TECHNIQUES FIGHTING TECHNIQUES FIGHTING TECHNI
NG TECHNIQUES FIGHTING TECHNIQUES FIGHTING TECHNIQUES FIGHTIN

24
Half-guard sweep 4

In this situation, Jean Jacques is underneath with Todd in his half-guard. Todd has his right elbow next to Jean Jacques's right ear, controlling his head. This is a classic half-guard side-control position. Jean Jacques uses the following clever and simple technique to apply so much pressure to Todd's groin and hips that he has to turn to release the pressure, giving up the reversal.

1 Todd is in Jean Jacques's half-guard with his right elbow blocking Jean Jacques's right ear. Jean Jacques has locked his legs around Todd's left leg in a figure-four to prevent him from passing the guard and scoring 3 points. Jean Jacques braces his left arm on Todd's right hip and slides his hips away to gain distance.

2 He then passes his right arm in front of Todd's chest until it comes out the other side.

3 At this point, Jean Jacques switches the legs, trapping Todd's left leg, and releases the figure-four. Notice that Jean Jacques continues to brace his left arm against Todd's right hip; otherwise, Todd will push his hips forward and flatten Jean Jacques's body against the mat.

4 Jean Jacques uses his right foot to trap Todd's left leg by planting it on the mat near the calf. As soon as he feels this control, Jean Jacques turns his body toward his left as if he wanted to lie on his stomach.

5 When Jean Jacques's torso is almost flat on the ground, his hips rotate toward the right and his right foot starts to pull Todd's left leg out. At this point, his right thigh applies a huge amount of pressure on Todd's hip and groin.

6 With so much force on his hips and groin, Todd has to turn and sit on the mat to release the pressure.

7 Jean Jacques continues to rotate toward his left until he ends up on top.

25

Half-guard sweep 5

Jean Jacques does not base his game on using the gi for position, but that doesn't mean he won't use it when opportunity presents itself. Here Jean Jacques makes clever use of Todd's gi skirt to launch him forward for the reversal. This technique is similar to position 21, except that here Todd keeps his body tight against Jean Jacques, preventing him from opening up the space necessary to slide his knee in (21.4) and create a barrier for Todd to push against. Since he is so close, Todd is simply pressing against Jean Jacques's chest.

1 Jean Jacques has Todd in his half-guard, and Todd is very close, pressing his chest against Jean Jacques. Jean Jacques uses his left hand to block Todd's attempt to grab around the neck with his right arm. Should that have occurred, Todd would have gained much more control of the position and made it much harder for Jean Jacques to escape. Jean Jacques is able to slide his right arm under Todd's left armpit.

2 Jean Jacques uses his left leg to bring his torso down, bringing his head down almost under Todd's hips. With his left hand, he grabs the collar of Todd's gi as close to the end as possible and gives it to his right hand. At this point, Todd's left leg is trapped by the combination of his own gi and Jean Jacques's arm. Notice that a constant feature of the half-guard sweeps is Jean Jacques's clever use of one leg (in this case, his left) to trap Todd's left leg. Many practitioners use both legs to keep the leg trapped. However, this technique hinders your movement because you cannot plant the right foot on the mat to help move your body.

IGHTING TECHNIQUES FIGHTING TECHNIQUES FIGHTING TECHNIQUES FI
NIQUES FIGHTING TECHNIQUES FIGHTING TECHNIQUES FIGHTING TECHN
ING TECHNIQUES FIGHTING TECHNIQUES FIGHTING TECHNIQUES FIGHTIN
ES FIGHTING TECHNIQUES FIGHTING TECHNIQUES FIGHTING TECHNIQUES
TECHNIQUES FIGHTING TECHNIQUES FIGHTING TECHNIQUES FIGHTING TI
GHTING TECHNIQUES FIGHTING TECHNIQUES FIGHTING TECHNIQUES FIGI

3 Pushing off his right foot, Jean Jacques executes a bridge to his left on his left shoulder as he extends his body and drives his right arm up, throwing Todd forward.

4 Jean Jacques plants his left elbow on the mat and props himself up. At this point, he has released the left leg trap over Todd's left leg and uses his right leg instead to trap the ankle as he starts to circle around Todd with his body. Jean Jacques does not have to worry about Todd escaping, because his grip on the gi collar gives him full control of the leg.

5 As he gets behind Todd and on top, Jean Jacques releases the right-hand grip on the collar and uses his right hand to grab around Todd's right thigh near the knee. Jean Jacques brings his left foot to his right knee, closing the noose on Todd's ankle, and drives his hips forward, pressing down on the knee as he pulls Todd's ankle back by straightening his leg. Jean Jacques also drives his chest forward onto Todd's hips, forcing him to fall to the right. Notice that the pressure generated by Jean Jacques's legs pulling Todd's ankle back and his hips pushing Todd's knee forward is enough to force Todd to roll over or submit to a knee bar.

6 Jean Jacques completes the reversal, landing on top of Todd in good position for a pass of his own.

26
Half-guard sweep 6

In this variation on position 25, Todd has planted his left arm out, got into base, lifted his hips and slipped his left knee over Jean Jacques's left thigh. With this small change, Todd has opened up numerous options for himself, none of which are good for Jean Jacques. Todd has, for example, sufficient leverage to execute a knee-through guard pass. If Jean Jacques tries to circle around Todd, as in the previous position, Todd will drive his left knee forward and pass the guard, or he may stand up. Depending on Jean Jacques's right leg position, Todd may also spin to his right and attempt a knee bar.

1 Just as Jean Jacques reached and got the gi collar with his right hand (25.2), Todd wisely planted his left arm out, opened his right leg, using it to raise his body, and slid his left knee over Jean Jacques's left thigh. Notice that Jean Jacques is trapping Todd's left ankle with his left leg.

2 Reverse Angle Jean Jacques hooks his right foot under Todd's left ankle and lifts it up. Now in full control of the ankle, Jean Jacques can release his own left foot trap over it.

2

NIQUES FIGHTING TECHNIQUES FIGHTING TECHNIQUES FIGHTING TECHNIQUES FIGHTING TECHNI
ING TECHNIQUES FIGHTING TECHNIQUES FIGHTING TECHNIQUES FIGHTING TECHNIQUES FIGHTIN
ES FIGHTING TECHNIQUES FIGHTING TECHNIQUES FIGHTING TECHNIQUES FIGHTING TECHNIQUES
TECHNIQUES FIGHTING TECHNIQUES FIGHTING TECHNIQUES FIGHTING TECHNIQUES FIGHTING TE
GHTIN FIGHTING TECHNIQUES FIGE
IQUES NIQUES FIGHTING TECHNI

3 Jean Jacques raises his right leg and opens his right elbow, driving his arm forward and forcing Todd to fall forward. At the same time, he used his left hand to block Todd's right knee.

4 As he releases the hook on Todd's left ankle, Jean Jacques grabs Todd's gi at the right knee with his left hand and Todd's right ankle with his right hand. Notice how tightly Jean Jacques's chest is pressing against Todd's left hip. This is very important as you don't want to give your opponent any space to evade the reversal. It is also important because the less extended your arms are, the greater the power you have to pull the knee in.

5 Jean Jacques switches his legs (see drill 2, pivoting the legs) and pushes off his toes. At the same time, he drives his chest forward onto Todd's hip while blocking Todd's right leg from opening up and bracing, thereby forcing Todd to roll to his right.

FIGHTING TECHNIQUES FIGHTING TECHNIQUES FIGHTING TECHNIQUES FIGHTING TECHNIQUES FIGHTI
FIGHTING TECHNIQUES FIGHTING TECHNIQUES FIGHTING TECHNIQUES FIGHTING TECHNIQUE
FIGHTING TECHNIQUES FIGHTING TECHNIQUES FIGHTING TECHNIQUES FIGHTING TE
FIGHTING TECHNIQUES FIGHTING TECHNIQUES FIGHTING TECHNIQUES FIO
FIGHTING TECHNIQUES FIGHTING TECHNIQUES FIGHTING TECHNIC
FIGHTING TECHNIQUES FIGHTING TECHNIQUES FIGHTING

27

Half-guard sweep 7: counter to the knee-across pass

Passing the half-guard by crossing the knee over the opponent's leg is a very common and powerful way to achieve the guard pass and earn 3 points. If not defended properly and early, the opponent will drive his knee across and use the leverage of his hips and back foot to release the trapped leg for the pass. In this technique, Jean Jacques not only avoids the pass, but sweeps the opponent and scores 2 points of his own for the reversal.

1 John is in Jean Jacques's half-guard. John's left arm is wrapped around Jean Jacques's head, controlling the upper body, while his right leg is trapped between Jean Jacques's legs. Jean Jacques braces his left hand on John's right biceps, thereby blocking John's right arm from getting under his left armpit for maximum control.

2 Since he cannot reach under Jean Jacques's left arm, John uses his right hand to grab the left knee as he raises his body and tries to pass his right knee across and over Jean Jacques's right leg for a knee-over pass. Jean Jacques counters this attempt by sliding his right hand under John's right leg and grabbing the right gi sleeve. Notice that Jean Jacques remained connected with John's right arm at all times with his left hand, which he used to deliver the sleeve to his right hand. Jean Jacques also changed his hips to his right and got under John's body. With his left foot he stepped on John's right foot and closed his knees around John's right knee to prevent him from turning the knee and getting it across. Since John's foot is glued to the ground, he cannot turn the knee to his left!

NIQUES FIGHTING TECHNIQUES FIGHTING TECHNIQUES FIGHTING TECHNI
ING TECHNIQUES FIGHTING TECHNIQUES FIGHTING TECHNIQUES FIGHTIN
ES FIGHTING TECHNIQUES FIGHTING TECHNIQUES FIGHTING TECHNIQUE
TECHNIQUES FIGHTING TECHNIQUES FIGHTING TECHNIQUES FIGHTING TE
GHTING TECHNIQUES FIGHTING TECHNIQUES FIGHTING TECHNIQUES FIGH
IQUES

3 Now in full control of John's right arm and leg, Jean Jacques opens his left leg while trapping John's leg with his right heel, plants his left foot on the mat, and uses it to turn his body to his left, causing John to fall to his right. Notice that John's right side is completely blocked and he cannot brace the fall.

4 Jean Jacques continues to turn to his own left, bringing John with him. As in all Brazilian jiu-jitsu moves, timing is very important. Jean Jacques needs to initiate the move and the reversal as soon as John raises his body and has his knee up to cross; it is at that point that he is vulnerable for the reversal. Should Jean Jacques wait too long, John can drop his weight back down, making it much harder for Jean Jacques to sweep him. Additionally, since Jean Jacques has pressed John's foot against the mat by stepping on it, John will have a much harder time sliding his foot back and dropping his weight even if he senses the sweep.

5 Jean Jacques continues to drive to his left, pulling John with him. Notice that he has his legs closed tightly against John's right leg the entire time to prevent him from stepping out.

6 Jean Jacques completes the reversal inside John's half-guard. He is now dominating his right arm and ready to pass.

TING TECHNIQUES FIGHTING TECHNIQUES FIGHTING TECHNIQUES FIGHTI
JES FIGHTING TECHNIQUES FIGHTING TECHNIQUES FIGHTING TECHNIQUE
TECHNIC FIGHTING TECHNIQUES FIGHTING TECHNIQUES FIGHTING TE
FIGHTING TECHNIQUES FIGHTING TECHNIQUES FIGHTING TECHNIQUES FI
NIQUES FIGHTING TECHNIQUES FIGHTING TECHNIQUES FIGHTING TECHNI
NG TECHNIQUES FIGHTING TECHNIQUES FIGHTING TECHNIQUES FIGHTIN

28

Half-guard sweep 8: taking the back

Jean Jacques has John in his cross guard, half-guard, or in the De La Riva guard. John is standing as he attempts a guard pass; if Jean Jacques doesn't counter, John will grab the knees and push them down to his own right and drive his left knee over Jean Jacques's left leg for the knee-over pass. In a match, passing the guard not only yields points, but also a strong controlling position in the side control or across-side. Jean Jacques, of course, does not want that. He not only has a reversal ready, but also takes the back for a full 6 points (2 for the reversal plus 4 for taking the back). In this demonstration, we start with the cross guard, but it could just as well be the De La Riva guard with Jean Jacques's right foot hooked under John's left thigh, or the half-guard with Jean Jacques's left arm wrapped inside John's right leg. The technique would be executed the same way.

1 Jean Jacques has John in his cross guard with both legs to one side and his knees close together, trapping John's left leg. His right hand controls John's left gi sleeve. John is standing and has his hands on Jean Jacques's knees. If Jean Jacques doesn't react, John will push them down to his right and drive his left knee over Jean Jacques's left leg, starting the knee-across pass.

2 While still holding John's sleeve, Jean Jacques releases his right leg and uses his left foot on John's buttocks to spin his body around until he can get his left hand on the outside of John's left ankle.

3 Jean Jacques crosses his feet again as he turns his body to his side and uses his left hand on John's ankle as a point to spin his body under John's legs.

4 As he continues to spin under John, Jean Jacques uses his right hand to grab inside John's right leg.

5 Jean Jacques then opens his legs up and throws them over his head, all the while turning under John. Notice that Jean Jacques's left leg is already hooked inside John's left leg. Jean continues to turn until he places his right foot inside John's right leg.

6 At this point, Jean Jacques is already under John with both his legs inside John's legs and his hands gripping the ankles. Jean Jacques has a lot of power in this position. As he drives his legs forward toward the mat, he will force John forward as well.

7 Jean Jacques releases John's ankles and grabs the back of his belt, pulling John down to him as he continues to kick his legs forward toward the mat.

8 John falls down on Jean Jacques's lap. Jean Jacques not only has the hooks in already, but is ready to attack the neck.

9 Jean Jacques releases his hands from John's belt and attacks the neck. At this point, he has scored 6 points, 2 for the reversal (as he was under John and now is on his back) and 4 more for taking the back with hooks.

FIGHTING TECHNIQUES FIGHTING TECHNIQUES FIGHTING TECHNIQUES FIGHTI
UES FIGHTING TECHNIQUES FIGHTING TECHNIQUES FIGHTING TECHNIQUE
TECHNIQUES FIGHTING TECHNIQUES FIGHTING TECHNIQUES FIGHTING TECHNIQUE
FIGHTING TECHNIQUES FIGHTING TECHNIQUES FIGHTING TECHNIQUES FIGHTING TE
GHTING TECHNIQUES FIGHTING TECHNIQUES FIGHTING TECHNIQUES FIGHTING TECHNIC
NIQUES FIGHTING TECHNIQUES FIGHTING TECHNIQUES FIGHTING TECHNI
NG TECHNIQUES FIGHTING TECHNIQUES FIGHTING TECHNIQUES FIGHTING
FIG

29

Half-guard sweep 8: taking the back (variation)

Here Jean Jacques demonstrates a variation of the previous position. In the previous position, Jean Jacques slid under John and forced him to fall on his lap as John tried to bring his weight down as a counter to the spin. This variation works best should John counter by standing up or moving forward.

1 As Jean Jacques spins under him to take the back, John stands upright and tries to walk forward.

2 Jean Jacques keeps his arms in front of John's ankles, preventing him from stepping forward, and kicks both legs hard toward the ground. His grip on John's ankles turns John's forward momentum into a forward fall.

FIGHTING TECHNIQUES FIGHTING TECHNIQUES FIGHTING TECHNIQUES FIGHTING TECHNI
NG TECHNIQUES FIGHTING TECHNIQUES FIGHTING TECHNIQUES FIGHTING TECHNI
NG TECHNIQUES FIGHTING TECHNIQUES FIGHTING TECHNIQUES FIGHTING TECHNIQUES FIGHTIN
S FIGHTING TECHNIQUES FIGHTING TECHNIQUES FIGHTING TECHNIQUES
TECHNIQUES FIGHTING TECHNIQUES FIGHTING TECHNIQUES FIGHTING T
HTING TE   NIQUES FIGH
IQUES FIGH   TING TECHNIQ
                                                                                       FIGHTING

3 Once John is on all fours, Jean Jacques puts his right foot down on the mat, releases his right hand, and grabs the back of John's belt. Notice that Jean Jacques's left leg still presses forward on John's left leg and his left hand lifts John's ankle to prevent him from using the leg to step up.

4 Pushing off his right leg, Jean Jacques pulls himself by John's belt and plants his left foot on the mat with his left calf tight on top of John's left leg to prevent him from stepping forward and standing up. His left hook is ready to go, requiring only that he throw his right leg over and hook the right foot.

30
Reversal from the half-guard: the classic sweep

The "classic" is a very beautiful and effective sweep from the half-guard. Once you achieve the position, the opponent is helpless for the sweep. The key to this technique is not to allow the opponent to grab your collar near your head. By controlling your opponent's arm and bringing it across your body, you gain control over him and set up the "classic."

1 Jean Jacques has John in his half-guard. He has trapped John's left leg between his legs. To keep John from achieving great control by using his right arm to grab Jean Jacques around his neck, Jean Jacques turns to his own left and intercepts John's right arm with his left hand. The technique can be executed if John already has his arm around Jean Jacques's neck, but Jean Jacques must first release that grip and bring John's arm around, as in step 2.

2 Jean Jacques reaches with his right hand to pull John's right arm across his body.

3 He then opens his legs, while keeping his left leg over John's left leg to deter him from passing the guard, and slides his hips away from John.

4 Jean Jacques continues to pull John's right arm across as he slides his right knee in front of John's hips and lassoes John's right leg with his left arm by wrapping it inside John's legs. Notice how John's upper body is twisted and his weight is on Jean Jacques's shin.

5 Jean Jacques starts to roll toward his right side as he pushes John's arm in, kicks his right leg out, and pulls on his left arm—completely turning John over his right shoulder. Notice that even though John attempts to brace with his left hand, he cannot stop the reversal over his right side. It is extremely important to continue to spin the opponent rather than simply try to roll him over; otherwise, his left arm brace will stop the move.

6 Jean Jacques continues to roll over the top of John. John has no way to brace and stop this move because he is being simultaneously rolled and spun.

7 Jean Jacques ends up on the opposite side in John's half-guard, and the reversal is completed.

FIGHTING TECHNIQUES FIGHTING TECHNIQUES FIGHTING TECHNIQUES FIGHTING TECHN
TING TECHNIQUES FIGHTING TECHNIQUES FIGHTING TECHNIQUES FIGHTI
UES FIGHTING TECHNIQUES FIGHTING TECHNIQUES FIGHTING TECHNIQUE
TECHNIQUES FIGHTING TECHNIQUES FIGHTING TECHNIQUES FIGHTING TE
FIGHTING TECHNIQUES FIGHTING TECHNIQUES FIGHTING TECHNIQUES FI
NIQUES FIGHTING TECHNIQUES FIGHTING TECHNIQUES FIGHTING TECHNI
ING TECHNIQUES FIGHTING TECHNIQUES FIGHTING TECHNIQUES FIGHTIN

31

Passing the half-guard 1: ballerina method

Being in someone's half-guard is so common in training and in competition that, as a competitor, you need to have a solid method of transposing the half-guard. When you want to score the points for passing the guard and then achieve across-side position to pursue a submission, Jean Jacques here demonstrates a very solid and effective way to do so.

1 Jean Jacques is in John's half-guard with his left leg trapped. He holds John's belt with his right hand, closes his right elbow next to John's ear to keep tight control of the head, and sits on his right hip. Although the position appears unstable for Jean Jacques, it is actually pretty solid, especially after he completes step 2.

2 While maintaining tight control over John's belt, Jean Jacques opens his lower (in this case, right) leg out and plants the toes on the mat. This not only gives him power to push forward onto John, but also helps him keep the position because he can brace any attempts to reverse him. He then slips his left arm inside John's legs under the right knee. This is one of the keys to this move, for as long as Jean Jacques has his arm under John's right leg, John cannot plant the right foot down on the mat to push himself over the top. Once he achieves this position, Jean Jacques waits for John to move.

FIGHTING TECHNIQUES FIGHTING TECHNIQUES FIGHTING TECHNIQUES FIG
NIQUES FIGHTING TECHNIQUES FIGHTING TECHNIQUES FIGHTING TECHNI
ING TECHNIQUES FIGHTING TECHNIQUES FIGHTING TECHNIQUES FIGHTIN
ES FIGHTING TECHNIQUES FIGHTING TECHNIQUES FIGHTING TECHNIQUES
TECHNIQUES FIGHTING TECHNIQUES FIGHTING TECHNIQUES FIGHTING TI
GHTIN   S FIGH
IQUES   ECHNIQ

3 Believing that he is stuck in a risky position, John opens his legs and attempt to plant his foot and roll over the top. Jean Jacques is in great control: his left arm prevents John's right leg from reaching the ground, effectively deterring any reversal; additionally, Jean Jacques's right leg, with the toes out and planted on the mat, gives him added balance.

4 As soon as he feels John's legs open, Jean Jacques circles his left leg out in a ballet-like move. His balance points are his right toe, his left arm under John's right leg, and his right elbow on the mat.

5 Still in balance, Jean Jacques continues circling the left leg until his foot touches the ground. At this point, he has great control of the position and his balance is impeccable.

6 Jean Jacques moves forward on John, driving off his legs to keep John's back on the mat and completing the guard pass.

32

Passing the half-guard 2: knee-push method

Here, Jean Jacques is inside John's half-guard, but this time John has his right arm over Jean Jacques's left arm, giving Jean Jacques greater control over John's upper body. Since he is in such good position, Jean Jacques will be more aggressive and use the knee-push method.

1 Jean Jacques is in John's half-guard and has his right arm wrapped around John's head and his left arm under John's right armpit; he has both hands clasped together in full control of John's upper body.

2 Jean Jacques releases his grip and uses his left hand to grab the right lapel of John's gi . . .

3 And give it to his right hand. Notice how tightly Jean Jacques holds John's lapel around the armpit. It is very important to get the grip right here for maximum control. A loose lapel will allow John to move his head and turn to his side. Jean Jacques, however, has the lapel cinched tightly around the armpit and drives his right shoulder onto John's chin, keeping his head immobile and, consequently, his back flat on the ground.

4 Jean Jacques slides his left arm inside John's leg just under his right knee. By doing this, Jean Jacques removes any chance of John opening his leg and exploding upward in an attempt to reverse the position.

FIGHTING TECHNIQUES FIGHTING TECHNIQUES FIGHTING TECHNIQUES FIGHTING TECHNIQUES
NIQUES FIGHTING TECHNIQUES FIGHTING TECHNIQUES FIGHTING TECHNIQUES FIGHTING TECHNI
ING TECHNIQUES FIGHTING TECHNIQUES FIGHTING TECHNIQUES FIGHTING TECHNIQUES FIGHTIN
ES FIGHTING TECHNIQUES FIGHTING TECHNIQUES FIGHTING TECHNIQUES FIGHTING TECHNIQUES
TECHNIQUES FIGHTING TECHNIQUES FIGHTING TECHNIQUES FIGHTING TECHNIQUES FIGHTING TE
GHTIN

5 Now in firm control of his balance, Jean Jacques drives John's legs toward the mat and raises his hips high enough to create space for his right knee to slide on top of John's stomach. Even though Jean Jacques's hips are up, his control over John's head and right leg prohibit John from executing a reversal.

6 Jean Jacques slides his right knee over John's stomach and pushes it forward, driving John's legs down as he slips his own leg out of the half-guard trap.

7 As he falls back with his right hip on the mat, Jean Jacques continues to drive his right knee forward on John's leg and pulls his left leg out. This is a very powerful move; John simply must let Jean Jacques remove his left leg.

8 As his foot comes out, Jean Jacques circles his left leg until the left foot touches the mat . . .

9 And switches his hips to be square with the ground.

107

FIGHTING TECHNIQUES FIGHTING TECHNIQUES FIGHTING TECHNIQUES FIGHTING TECHN
TING TECHNIQUES FIGHTING TECHNIQUES FIGHTING TECHNIQUES FIGHTI
UES FIGHTING TECHNIQUES FIGHTING TECHNIQUES FIGHTING TECHNIQUE
TECHNI FIGHTING TECHNIQUES FIGHTING TECHNIQUES FIGHTING TE
FIGHTING TECHNIQUES FIGHTING TECHNIQUES FIGHTING TECHNIQUES FI
NIQUES FIGHTING TECHNI
ING TECHNIQUES FIGHTIN

33

Passing the half-guard 3: knee-through method

This option for passing the half-guard starts much like the previous technique, with Jean Jacques in John's half-guard and his left leg trapped inside John's legs. We pick up at step 32.4, where Jean Jacques already slipped his right knee on John's stomach. In this case, John has some freedom to move his head, as Jean Jacques's lapel grip is, for some reason, not as tight. John has turned his legs to the left, and Jean Jacques understands that if he escapes his legs, John could follow him and turn into him for a reversal.

1 Jean Jacques has control of John's lapel under the armpit with his right hand and his left arm inside John's leg under the right knee. He has also slipped his right knee over John's stomach, but John has been able to turn to his own left a little, and Jean Jacques chooses to use the knee-through technique.

2 Jean Jacques grips John's right gi sleeve with his left hand and pulls it up, simultaneously driving his right knee across John's stomach until it touches the mat on the opposite side. This forces John's body flat on the ground, thus preventing him from turning to his left and possibly reversing Jean Jacques. Notice the tremendous control that Jean Jacques has over John and how awkward John's body is. Jean Jacques has the lapel control under the armpit, his left hand pulls John's right sleeve up, and his knee drives John's legs down! The pressure in the position is tremendous.

3 Jean Jacques applies the pressure and slips his left leg out. Notice that he keeps his right hip pressing against John's stomach, and his right foot is hooked on John's left thigh. Jean Jacques plants his left foot out, leg open for balance, and his hands pull the lapel and sleeve.

4 Jean Jacques slides his right leg through until his right knee is almost touching John's right shoulder, ending up with the guard passed and in a great side-control position, controlling the head and the opposite sleeve.

34

Passing the half-guard submission option: armlock

Because being in someone's half-guard is almost as prevalent as being in someone's guard in Brazilian jiu-jitsu, it is vital to know a few ways to pass the half-guard or otherwise change the circumstances. The previous 3 positions demonstrate excellent techniques for simply passing the half-guard, but of course Jean Jacques prefers to go for the kill whenever possible. Many people assume they are safe from being submitted from the half-guard. Here, Jean Jacques demonstrates a way to go directly from the half-guard to the armlock.

1 Jean Jacques is in John's half-guard with his left leg trapped by John's legs. Jean Jacques's left arm underhooks John's right arm near the armpit as he attempts to pass, perhaps using the underhook/knee-through method. Normally, Jean Jacques would use his right arm to block John's head, preventing John from turning into him, as he is here. Because Jean Jacques wants to take John's arm, however, he encourages John to turn in by not blocking the head with his right arm and by removing the pressure of his left shoulder on John's right shoulder.

2 Jean Jacques plants his right hand on the mat and props his body up, lifting his hips. Since he had underhooked John's right arm with his left arm, Jean Jacques already has the control necessary for the armlock. He extends his left leg and slides it out until the only thing caught in John's legs is the ankle. When this happens, there will be enough space for Jean Jacques to circle his right knee around John's head.

NIQUES FIGHTING TECHNIQUES FIGHTING TECHNIQUES FIGHTING TECHNI
ING TECHNIQUES FIGHTING TECHNIQUES FIGHTING TECHNIQUES FIGHTIN
ES FIGHTING TECHNIQUES FIGHTING TECHNIQUES FIGHTING TECHNIQUES
TECHNIQUES FIGHTING TECHNIQUES FIGHTING TECHNIQUES FIGHTING TI
GHTIN   ES FIGH
IQUES   ECHNIQ
NG T   GHTING

3 Pivoting on his right hand, Jean Jacques continues to move his body around John's head. Notice that Jean Jacques's ankle is still trapped inside John's leg, so technically John still has the half-guard and believes himself somewhat safe.

4 As his hips pass John's head, Jean Jacques starts to slide his right knee in toward John's back and sits down on the mat. Notice that Jean Jacques's left leg is over John's head.

5 Jean Jacques sits down on the mat and opens his right leg, still using his right hand and arm to keep his balance.

6 Jean Jacques loops his right leg over John's chest and pulls down on the right arm with his chest and left arm for the armlock. His ankle is still trapped in John's legs, but that does not affect the lock.

7 Jean Jacques finishes the armlock as he extends his body, pushing his hips against John's right elbow. At this point, John has to release the trap over Jean Jacques's left ankle, but even if he didn't he'd still be submitted.

FIGHTING TECHNIQUES FIGHTING TECHNIQUES FIGHTING TECHNIQUES FIGHTI
ES FIGHTING TECHNIQUES FIGHTING TECHNIQUES FIGHTING TECHNIQUE
TECHNIQUES FIGHTING TECHNIQUES FIGHTING TECHNIQUES FIGHTING TE
FIGHTING TECHNIQUES FIGHTING TECHNIQUES FIGHTING TECHNIQUES FI
NIQUES FIGHTING TECHNIQUES FIGHTING TECHNIQUES FIGHTING TECHNI
NG TECHNIQUES FIGHTING TECHNIQUES FIGHTING TECHNIQUES FIGHTIN

35

Guard pass: toreana

In Brazilian jiu-jitsu it seem that you spend half the time defending the guard and the other half trying to pass someone's guard. These two situations are arguably the most fundamental of the elements of Brazilian jiu-jitsu. When it comes to competition especially, you cannot be very successful if you don't have a strong guard pass in your arsenal. The toreana (bullfighter) guard pass is a very effective method of passing the guard, especially when the opponent has great flexibility. The common stacking method (shown in position 56, in which you use your grip on the collar and belt to drive the opponent's legs over his head, "stacking" him) is less effective against a fighter who is flexible enough to be comfortable when stacked upside down, because he will simply keep finding ways to bring his legs in front of the passer's body. In such cases, the toreana is particularly useful, as it deals with the legs right away. The problem with the toreana is that sometimes the opponent sits up as you start to pass, making it easier for him to block, escape the hips, and defend the pass. Jean Jacques uses his shoulder to keep John flat on the mat and complete the pass.

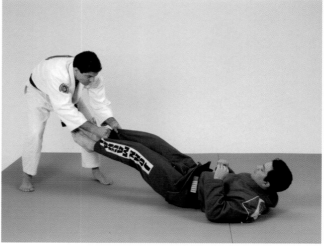

1 Jean Jacques is attempting to pass John's guard. He has control of John's gi pants near the shin. Note that if Jean Jacques were to hold at the knees, he would allow John to circle his feet over his arm and take away the control. Jean Jacques keeps his elbows closed to prevent John's feet from reaching his biceps for the spider guard position.

2 Jean Jacques takes a step back with each leg as he pulls John's legs with him and stretches them, driving them to the mat.

NIQUES FIGHTING TECHNIQUES FIGHTING TECHNIQUES FIGHTING TECHNI
ING TECHNIQUES FIGHTING TECHNIQUES FIGHTING TECHNIQUES FIGHTIN
ES FIGHTING TECHNIQUES FIGHTING TECHNIQUES FIGHTING TECHNIQUES
TECHNIQUES FIGHTING TECHNIQUES FIGHTING TECHNIQUES FIGHTING TE
GHTIN   ES FIGH
IQUES   ECHNIC

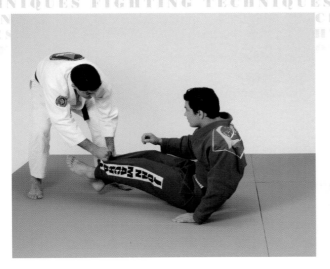

3 Knowing that Jean Jacques wants to pin his legs on the mat for the toreana, John immediately sits up so he can both block Jean Jacques's pass and be able to escape his hips to prevent Jean Jacques from reaching his right side.

4 Jean Jacques pins John's legs on the mat by placing his weight on his hands, and walks around to John's side, leading with his left shoulder. It is extremely important not to let go of the legs as you walk around to your opponent's side, or he will just coil his legs, scoot his hips, and replace the guard. His movement to replace is a lot shorter than the one you are executing to come around to his side!

5 Leading with his shoulder and the side of his body, Jean Jacques pushes John's torso back down to the mat. Notice that he still has a firm grip on John's legs and actually stretches them out with his arms straight, making it very hard for John to replace the guard.

6 Jean Jacques continues driving his body, flattening John. Once his hips and John's back hits the mat, Jean Jacques lets go of his left-hand grip on John's right leg and grabs the left hip while placing his elbow next to John's torso for the guard pass.

TING TECHNIQUES FIGHTING TECHNIQUES FIGHTING TECHNIQUES FIGHTI
UES FIGHTING TECHNIQUES FIGHTING TECHNIQUES FIGHTING TECHNIQUE
TECHNI FIGHTING TECHNIQUES FIGHTING TECHNIQUES FIGHTING TE
FIGHTING TECHNIQUES FIGHTING TECHNIQUES FIGHTING TECHNIQUES FI
NIQUES FIGHTING TECHNIQUES FIGHTING TECHNIQUES FIGHTING TECHNI
ING TECHNIQUES FIGHTING TECHNIQUES FIGHTING TECHNIQUES FIGHTIN

36
Guard pass: spinning toreana

Here Jean Jacques demonstrates a great variation of the standing toreana called the spinning toreana. Standing guard passes are very useful against guard fighters who are very active with their legs, using hooks and sitting sweeps, so you should master this position.

1 Jean Jacques is attempting to pass John's guard. Notice that he is standing up to avoid John's hooks and sweeps. His right hand pushes down on John's left leg, and his right knee pushes against the back of John's left thigh for two reasons: 1) to keep John from grapevining his leg around Jean Jacques's right leg, and 2) to keep John from putting his left foot on the biceps for a spider guard position. Jean Jacques's left hand grabs John's right gi pants at the knee.

2 Jean Jacques switches his right hand from John's left knee to the right one and pushes that leg down to the mat with both hands. He uses both hands to be certain that he can control the leg (legs are more powerful than arms). Notice how Jean Jacques continues to drive his right knee into the back of John's leg.

3 Once he has John's right leg on the mat, Jean Jacques puts all his weight on the grip and uses it to pivot his body around John's left leg. At this point, John uses both arms to push, attempting to stop Jean Jacques from coming to his side.

NIQUES FIGHTING TECHNIQUES FIGHTING TECHNIQUES FIGHTING TECHN
ING TECHNIQUES FIGHTING TECHNIQUES FIGHTING TECHNIQUES FIGHTIN
ES FIGHTING TECHNIQUES FIGHTING TECHNIQUES FIGHTING TECHNIQUES
TECHNIQUES FIGHTING TECHNIQUES FIGHTING TECHNIQUES FIGHTING TI
GHTING TECHNIQUES FIGHTING TECHNIQUES FIGHTING TECHNIQUES FIGH
IQUES FIGHTING TECHNIQUES FIGHTING TECHNIQUES FIGHTING TECHNI

4 Sensing the block on his right arm, Jean Jacques loops his right leg over John's body while still pinning John's right knee to the mat.

5 Jean Jacques plants his right foot on the left side of John's body. Notice that to this point he hasn't released the pressure on John's right knee. Otherwise, John would be able to replace the guard by throwing that leg over Jean Jacques's shoulder.

6 Still keeping his weight on John's right leg, Jean Jacques lowers his body on top of John's left leg and flattens it. Jean Jacques will now simply drop his weight on top of John and adjust his hands for side control.

FIGHTING TECHNIQUES FIGHTING TECHNIQUES FIGHTING TECHNIQUES FIGHTI
ES FIGHTING TECHNIQUES FIGHTING TECHNIQUES FIGHTING TECHNIQUE
FIGHTING TECHNIQUES FIGHTING TECHNIQUES FIGHTING TE
FIGHTING TECHNIQUES FIGHTING TECHNIQUES FIGHTING TECHNIQUES FI
FIGHTING TECHNIQUE FIGHTING TECHNIQUES FIGHTING TECHNI
TECHNIQUES FIGHTING TECHNIQUES FIGHTING TECHNIQUES FIGHTIN

37

Spider guard pass: one-hand toreana

The spider guard is very common and effective and is used often to stall in tournaments. With both feet on the biceps and control of the sleeves, it is also very effective in sweeps and triangle set-ups. Having a few options to deal with this guard is a must for competition success. In this case, John demonstrates a clever and quick variation of the toreana pass.

1 Jean Jacques has John in his spider guard with both his feet pressing against John's biceps while at the same time controlling both sleeves with his hands.

2 John's first objective is to release one side from Jean Jacques's control. It is very hard to pry your arm free of the pressure applied here by Jean Jacques's legs. Instead of fighting against it, John simply circles his left hand under Jean Jacques's right leg and deflects the foot on his left bicep with his left forearm pushing up. Now Jean Jacques has pressure on John's right side only.

NIQUES FIGHTING TECHNIQUES FIGHTING TECHNIQUES FIGHTING TECHNI
ING TECHNIQUES FIGHTING TECHNIQUES FIGHTING TECHNIQUES FIGHTIN
ES FIGHTING TECHNIQUES FIGHTING TECHNIQUES FIGHTING TECHNIQUE
TECHNIQUES FIGHTING TECHNIQUES FIGHTING TECHNIQUES FIGHTING TE
GHTIN   FIGHTING TECHNIQUES FIGH
IQUES   CHNIQUES FIGHTING TECHNI

3 As soon as he releases the pressure to one side, John twists his body to his left, flexing his left knee and straightening his right leg as he drives Jean Jacques's left leg over his right one and down toward the mat. With nothing to brace on, Jean Jacques cannot stop this motion.

4 John pins Jean Jacques's left leg over his right as he steps right toward Jean Jacques's head and cinches his hips to Jean Jacques's. At this point, John's left hand should control either Jean Jacques's left elbow or his left hip to prevent Jean Jacques from rolling to his right and achieving the all-fours position to defend the guard pass.

5 John circles his right arm around Jean Jacques's head until he holds the right shoulder. Notice how tight John is to Jean Jacques, thus denying him the space to replace the guard with the knee. Also notice that John controls Jean Jacques's left arm to keep him from rolling over to his knees.

117

TING TECHNIQUES FIGHTING TECHNIQUES FIGHTING TECHNIQUES FIGHTI
UES FIGHTING TECHNIQUES FIGHTING TECHNIQUES FIGHTING TECHNIQUE
TECHNI FIGHTING TECHNIQUES FIGHTING TECHNIQUES FIGHTING TE
FIGHTING TECHNIQUES FIGHTING TECHNIQUES FIGHTING TECHNIQUES FI
NIQUES FIGHTING TECHNIQUES FIGHTING TECHNIQUES FIGHTING TECHNI
ING TECHNIQUES FIGHTING TECHNIQUES FIGHTING TECHNIQUES FIGHTIN

38

Spider guard pass: one-hand toreana (variation)

In this variation, instead of pivoting his body to his left, John actually walks around to his left to pin Jean Jacques's left leg over his right. Which technique you choose is a matter of preference, as both methods work well, but this technique is especially useful against fighters with longer legs. Applying the spin technique against them risks ending up too far down to be able to trap the hips with your hips. If your opponent has long legs or tries to recenter his hips by walking around to the left, this variation will enable you to gain the necessary angle to pin one leg over the other.

1 John has already circled his left hand around Jean Jacques's right leg and released the pressure of the foot on his biceps. At this point, John's right hand holds Jean Jacques's left gi pants at the shin, and Jean Jacques is holding John's right sleeve.

2 John walks to his left, lowering his upper body while forcing Jean Jacques's left leg down.

3 John continues driving and pins Jean Jacques's left leg over his right, trapping him. John has his weight on his right hand to keep Jean Jacques's leg pinned to the mat.

FIGHTING TECHNIQUES FIGHTING TECHNIQUES FIGHTING TECHNIQUES FIG
NIQUES FIGHTING TECHNIQUES FIGHTING TECHNIQUES FIGHTING TECHNI
ING TECHNIQUES FIGHTING TECHNIQUES FIGHTING TECHNIQUES FIGHTIN
ES FIGHTING TECHNIQUES FIGHTING TECHNIQUES FIGHTING TECHNIQUES
TECHNIQUES FIGHTING TECHNIQUES FIGHTING TECHNIQUES FIGHTING TI
GHTING TECHNIQUES FIGHTING TECHNIQUES FIGHTING TECHNIQUES FIGH
IQUES FIGHTING TECHNIQUES FIGHTING TECHNIQUES FIGHTING TECHNIQ

4 John braces with his left hand on the mat and lowers his right shoulder onto Jean Jacques's hip while still controlling the left gi pants. John now has Jean Jacques's hips and legs trapped.

5 Placing his weight on the left hand and right shoulder, John thrusts his legs upward.

6 With his legs in the air, John turns his body to his right and lands next to Jean Jacques's back. Notice that John still maintains control over Jean Jacques's left leg and continues to use his right shoulder to pressure Jean Jacques's left hip to prevent him from turning or escaping the hips.

7 John wraps his right arm around Jean Jacques's head and grabs the right shoulder. With his left hand, he grabs Jean Jacques's right sleeve, pulls it toward him, and places his left elbow on Jean Jacques's hip, preventing him from rolling to his knees.

39

Guard pass: toreana step-through directly to knee-on–stomach

When attempting to pass someone's guard while standing, you will often have the opportunity to go one step further. Here, the opening occurs when John relaxes his legs, allowing Jean Jacques to force them apart instead of driving both legs together straight down to the mat or to the side (as in the traditional toreana).

1 Jean Jacques is standing as he attempts to pass John's guard. He is using the toreana method because John is very adept at using his feet as hooks. Jean Jacques holds John's legs below the knees with his hands.

2 John's legs are relaxed, allowing Jean Jacques to pull them apart. He steps to his right with his right foot and drives his body weight through his right arm, forcing John's left leg to the mat while he keeps the right leg open with his left arm.

FIGHTING TECHNIQUES FIGHTING TECHNIQUES FIGHTING TECHNIQUES FIG
NIQUES FIGHTING TECHNIQUES FIGHTING TECHNIQUES FIGHTING TECHNI
ING TECHNIQUES FIGHTING TECHNIQUES FIGHTING TECHNIQUES FIGHTIN
ES FIGHTING TECHNIQUES FIGHTING TECHNIQUES FIGHTING TECHNIQUES
TECHNIQUES FIGHTING TECHNIQUES FIGHTING TECHNIQUES FIGHTING TI
GHTIN
IQI ES

3 Jean Jacques steps through John's legs with his left leg and plants his left foot right next to John's left hip to keep him from centering his body by scooting his hips to his left. Notice that Jean Jacques still controls John's legs with his hands.

4 Jean Jacques steps over John's leg with his right leg as he leans forward, driving his left knee across John's stomach. Notice that Jean Jacques has not released his grip on John's legs; otherwise, John would be able to either replace the guard or roll onto all fours to avoid the guard pass.

5 Jean Jacques pushes his left knee on the right side of John's stomach and achieves the knee-on-stomach position.

40

Guard pass: over-the-leg toreana

Another very effective guard pass for tournaments is the over-the-leg toreana. Much like the traditional toreana, this technique is a good option against a defender with exceptional hooks and active legs. Also like the traditional toreana, the passer here controls both of the opponent's legs, but then opts to lock one leg to the mat, leaving the other one out. As in position 39, Jean Jacques attempts to step through John's legs, but John has his arms out ready to block. Jean Jacques goes for the over-the-leg option.

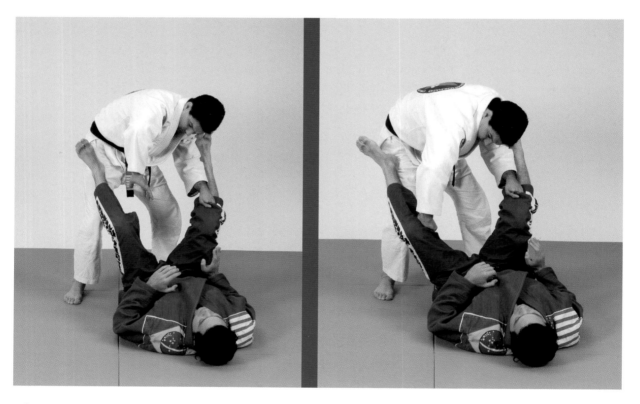

1 Jean Jacques is attempting to pass John's guard by holding John's right leg with his left hand grabbing near the knee. He turns his right hand back (thumb pointing in) to grip John's left leg.

NIQUES FIGHTING TECHNIQUES FIGHTING TECHNIQUES FIGHTING TECHNI
ING TECHNIQUES FIGHTING TECHNIQUES FIGHTING TECHNIQUES FIGHTIN
S FIGHTING TECHNIQUES FIGHTING TECHNIQUES FIGHTING TECHNIQUES
TECHNIQUES FIGHTING TECHNIQUES FIGHTING TECHNIQUES FIGHTING TE
HTING TECHNIQUES FIGHTING TECHNIQUES FIGHTING TECHNIQUES FIGH
IQUES FIGHTING TECHNIQUES FIGHTING TECHNIQUES FIGHTING TECHNIQ

2 Having achieved a firm grip of the legs, Jean Jacques pushes John's left leg to the mat and keeps the right one up and open. John sees the opening inside his legs and readies to block Jean Jacques's pass with his arms.

3 Jean Jacques walks to his own right and steps over John's left leg. Notice that had Jean Jacques used the normal grip with the thumbs pointing up on his right, he would have twisted his own wrist!

4 As soon as he reaches John's side, Jean Jacques drops his body down and drives his forehead into John's right shoulder, pushing him flat to the mat.

5 Jean Jacques releases his grip on the legs and circles his right arm around John's head to complete the guard pass.

41
Guard pass: over-the-leg toreana (opponent reacts)

Here Jean Jacques attempts to use the over-the-leg toreana, but as soon as he reaches John's side, John reacts by pushing his hips in, effectively blocking Jean Jacques's path. It is possible that either Jean Jacques did not fully control John's legs or that John has powerful legs. Regardless, Jean Jacques is ready and goes to the other side.

1 Jean Jacques is passing around to his right. He pushes John's left leg to the mat as he opens the right one. At this point, John reacts by planting his left toes on the mat and curling his right leg.

2 Pushing off his left foot, John brings his hips to his left and faces Jean Jacques, blocking the pass to that side. If Jean Jacques doesn't react, John will either sit up or place his foot on Jean Jacques's hip or hook it inside the legs for guard work.

FIGHTING TECHNIQUES FIGHTING TECHNIQUES FIGHTING TECHNIQUES FIGHTING TECHNI
NIQUES FIGHTING TECHNIQUES FIGHTING TECHNIQUES FIGHTING TECHNIQUES FIGHTING TECHNI
ING TECHNIQUES FIGHTING TECHNIQUES FIGHTING TECHNIQUES FIGHTING TECHNIQUES FIGHTIN
ES FIGHTING TECHNIQUES FIGHTING TECHNIQUES FIGHTING TECHNIQUES FIGHTING TECHNIQUES
TECHNIQUES FIGHTING TECHNIQUES FIGHTING TECHNIQUES FIGHTING TECHNIQUES FIGHTING TE
GHTING TECH   CHNIQUES FIGH
IQUES FIGHT   TING TECHNIQ

3 Jean Jacques, however, uses John's motion and twists John's legs around counterclockwise, pushing the left leg up and the right one down.

4 With his right leg, Jean Jacques steps over John's right leg, then releases his left-hand grip on John's right leg and goes directly for the knee-on-stomach, sliding his right knee across John's stomach.

42

Guard pass: leg-and-arm grab

Having a variety of solid guard passes for every situation is a huge advantage for a serious competitor and Brazilian jiu-jitsu practitioner. Jean Jacques here demonstrates a great way to pass when your opponent's legs are high.

1 Jean Jacques grabs John's left arm with his right arm and John's left leg with his left hand. If John doesn't react, Jean Jacques will simply jump up and turn John's body to his right and pass to the left, as shown in the next technique.

2 Pushing off his right leg, John counters by turning his body to his left, sliding his left knee in front of Jean Jacques's hip, and looping his right leg over Jean Jacques's head.

3 Jean Jacques spreads his knees and drops his torso. With his left arm, he wraps John's left leg in front of his left shin and grabs around the left knee, as if he were hugging the leg. Jean Jacques pulls John's left arm with his right hand.

FIGHTING TECHNIQUES FIGHTING TECHNIQUES FIGHTING TECHNIQUES FIGHTING TECHNIQUES FIGHTING TECHNI
NIQUES FIGHTING TECHNIQUES FIGHTING TECHNIQUES FIGHTING TECHNIQUES FIGHTING TECHNI
ING TECHNIQUES FIGHTING TECHNIQUES FIGHTING TECHNIQUES FIGHTING TECHNIQUES FIGHTIN
ES FIGHTING TECHNIQUES FIGHTING TECHNIQUES FIGHTING TECHNIQUES FIGHTING TECHNIQUES
TECHNIQUES FIGHTING TECHNIQUES FIGHTING TECHNIQUES FIGHTING TECHNIQUES FIGHTING TE
GHTING TECHNIQUES FIGHTING TECHNIQUES FIGHTING TECHNIQUES FIGHTING TECHNIQUES FIGH
IQUES FIGHTING TECHNIQUES FIGHTING TECHNIQUES FIGHTING TECHNIQUES FIGHTING TECHNIQ

4 Jean Jacques drives his body forward, using his chest to push John's legs to his right.

5 Jean Jacques continues to extend his body. He thrusts his hips forward and arches his torso up, releasing the block from John's left shin.

6 Jean Jacques reaches across the side position as he extends John's left leg down with his left arm and pins John's right arm to the mat with his right hand. Notice Jean Jacques's hips pressing forward and down on John's side, keeping John pinned under him.

43

Guard pass: leg-and-arm grab (jump up)

A great variation of the leg-and-arm pass is shown here. In this situation, Jean Jacques opts to spring to his feet and go directly for the knee-on-stomach because John's legs are low. If Jean Jacques tries to use technique 42, he will fail because he will not be able to drive John's legs away by extending his body. He opts instead to spring to his feet.

1 Jean Jacques has his left arm wrapped around John's left leg, grabbing the outside of the thigh just above the knee. His right hand is pulling on John's left arm, but this time as he tries to extend his body, he notices that John is turned too far to his left and his legs are too close to the mat. This position makes it very difficult for Jean Jacques to use his torso to push John's legs away.

2 Jean Jacques jumps to his feet while still holding on to John's left leg and arm.

NIQUES FIGHTING TECHNIQUES FIGHTING TECHNIQUES FIGHTING TECHNI
ING TECHNIQUES FIGHTING TECHNIQUES FIGHTING TECHNIQUES FIGHTIN
ES FIGHTING TECHNIQUES FIGHTING TECHNIQUES FIGHTING TECHNIQUES
TECHNIQUES FIGHTING TECHNIQUES FIGHTING TECHNIQUES FIGHTING TE
GHTING TECHNIQUES FIGHTING TECHNIQUES FIGHTING TECHNIQUES FIGH
IQUES FIGHTING

3 Jean Jacques extends his body and pulls up on John's left arm and leg, rolling him to his right. Notice that Jean Jacques is not lifting John off the ground. He just pulls up on the left side.

4 Jean Jacques steps forward with his left leg, continues to turn John over to his right, and slides his left knee onto John's left ribcage for the pass to the knee-on-stomach.

TING TECHNIQUES FIGHTING TECHNIQUES FIGHTING TECHNIQUES FIGHTING TECHN
ES FIGHTING TECHNIQUES FIGHTING TECHNIQUES FIGHTING TECHNIQUES FIGHTI
ECHNIQUES FIGHTING TECHNIQUES FIGHTING TECHNIQUES FIGHTING TECHNIQUE
IGHTING TECHNIQUES FIGHTING TECHNIQUES FIGHTING TECHNIQUES FIGHTING TE
NIQUES FIGHTING TECHNIQUES FIGHTING TECHNIQUES FIGHTING TECHNIQUES FI
ING TECHNIQUES FIGHTING TECHNIQUES FIGHTING TECHNIQUES FIGHTING TECHNI
ING TECHNIQUES FIGHTING TECHNIQUES FIGHTING TECHNIQUES FIGHTING

44

Spider guard pass to armlock

John loves to use this technique for the spider guard pass. Since the opponent is so bent on controlling the arm with his hands and feet on the biceps, John releases one side and uses the same principle as in the previous guard pass of extending and exposing one side to take the arm.

1 Jean Jacques has John in his spider guard. His feet are pushing on John's biceps and his hands are gripping the gi sleeves for a classic spider guard position.

2 Since Jean Jacques controls the gi sleeve, he cannot stop John from simply circling his wrist around. John circles his left hand around Jean Jacques's left leg and flicks his elbow in, releasing Jean Jacques's right foot from his biceps.

3 John reaches with his left hand and grabs the inside of Jean Jacques's left leg near the ankle.

FIGHTING TECHNIQUES FIGHTING TECHNIQUES FIGHTING TECHNIQUES FI
NIQUES FIGHTING TECHNIQUES FIGHTING TECHNIQUES FIGHTING TECHNI
ING TECHNIQUES FIGHTING TECHNIQUES FIGHTING TECHNIQUES FIGHTIN
ES FIGHTING TECHNIQUES FIGHTING TECHNIQUES FIGHTING TECHNIQUES
TECHNIQUES FIGHTING TECHNIQUES FIGHTING TECHNIQUES FIGHTING TE
GHTING TECHNIQUES FIGHTING TECHNIQUES FIGHTING TECHNIQUES FIGH
IQUES

4 John extends his body and pulls Jean Jacques's left leg and arm with him, exposing his left side as he steps in with his left leg.

5 John pulls Jean Jacques's left arm up and pushes Jean Jacques's left leg away as he turns Jean Jacques on his side and slides his left knee on Jean Jacques's stomach. Notice that John turned Jean Jacques slightly around clockwise by twisting his arms. This makes it easier to pass the leg over for the armlock.

6 Without releasing the pull on Jean Jacques's arm and leg, John bends his knees and steps over Jean Jacques's head with his right leg, making sure his hips are pressing against Jean Jacques's left arm below the elbow.

7 John drops down to the mat for the armlock and lifts his hips, thereby extending Jean Jacques's left elbow.

TING TECHNIQUES FIGHTING TECHNIQUES FIGHTING TECHNIQUES FIGHTI
UES FIGHTING TECHNIQUES FIGHTING TECHNIQUES FIGHTING TECHNIQUE
TECHNI FIGHTING TECHNIQUES FIGHTING TECHNIQUES FIGHTING TE
FIGHTING TECHNIQUES FIGHTING TECHNIQUES FIGHTING TECHNIQUES FI
NIQUES FIGHTING TECHNIQUES FIGHTING TECHNIQUES FIGHTING TECHNI
ING TECHNIQUES FIGHTING TECHNIQUES FIGHTING TECHNIQUES FIGHTIN

45
Guard pass variation

John demonstrates a guard pass from a different position, using the same grab-and-spread principle. In this case, he is passing Jean Jacques's open guard with the arm under the leg, but Jean Jacques manages to get one end of the spider guard in.

1 John is attempting to pass Jean Jacques's guard. His right arm controls Jean Jacques's leg, grabbing it around the knee. Jean Jacques has his right foot on John's biceps, and his right hand grips John's left gi sleeve.

2 John moves his right hand from Jean Jacques's knee to his left arm and opens it up. As he opens, he also drives his right shoulder up, forcing Jean Jacques's left leg over to John's left. With his left hand, John pushes down on Jean Jacques's right leg. This entire motion is like turning a large wheel to the left, as John's left hand goes down and his right arm circles up.

3 John steps up with his right leg and continues turning Jean Jacques. John maintains the same circular motion with his arms, his left hand pushing Jean Jacques's right leg down to the mat and his right arm pulling Jean Jacques's left arm up.

4 Once he has reached Jean Jacques's side, John kneels down with his right knee . . .

5 And achieves the across-side position with his right arm around Jean Jacques's head and his left arm in front of Jean Jacques's body, left elbow on the mat and left hand grabbing the right shoulder.

46

Guard pass: "stacking" method with knee-through

Serious competitors simply cannot know too many guard passes. Scoring the points for the guard pass and attaining such a stable and offensive position as the side control is tantamount to winning the fight. Here Jean Jacques demonstrates a variation of the traditional guard pass called the stacking method. In the stacking method, the passer reaches with his arm under the defender's leg and grabs the defender's opposite collar while controlling the hip with his other hand, "stacking" the defender onto himself as he drives the leg or legs over the head and passes to the side of the trapped leg. The option to pass with the knee inside is used when the opponent blocks the passer's hips, giving him two options to pass. In this case, however, John reacts and blocks Jean Jacques's knee so Jean uses the third option, which is changing the knee inside.

1 Jean Jacques attempts to pass John's guard using the stacking method, but John has already blocked Jean Jacques's hips, forcing him to go inside. Notice Jean Jacques's left hand gripping John's left collar around the right leg and his right hand pushing down on John's left leg. Since he was blocked on the outside, Jean Jacques opts to pass on the inside. His right knee is over John's left leg with his right foot hooked over to prevent John from using it to trap Jean Jacques's left leg, thereby putting him in the half-guard. Jean Jacques proceeds, driving his torso inside John's legs. John reacts by turning his body to his left to block the pass.

2 John places both arms straight, pushing Jean Jacques's right knee away and blocking the path for the pass. At this point, Jean Jacques has two options: 1) to go back and try passing on the outside, and 2) to slide the other knee through. He opts for that because John was able to get some separation by pushing his knee away.

3 Jean Jacques continues to hold and stack John's left leg and slides his left knee in the space created by John pushing his right knee away. Notice that Jean Jacques continues to hold John's left gi pants as he pushes down on that leg.

4 Once he has both his knees inside and over John's left leg, Jean Jacques releases his right hand grip . . .

5 And loops his right arm around John's head as he releases his right foot hook on John's leg and drives his chest to John's chest. Jean Jacques still holds John's gi collar with his left hand, keeping control over John's hip movement.

6 With his right hand, Jean Jacques grabs John's right shoulder around John's head. He releases his left foot hook over John's leg and presses his chest on John's chest, turning him to his right and forcing his back flat on the mat for across-side control. Notice that Jean Jacques brings his left knee tight on John's left hip to keep him from sliding his leg in and replacing the guard.

47

Guard pass submission option 1: knee lock

Jean Jacques and John both prefer to submit opponents than to score points. Although each has his own vision of how to achieve that goal, their games are both clearly directed toward the quick finish. In this technique, John demonstrates one of his favorite submissions, the knee bar while passing the guard. This technique can be applied in many variations; a common one is demonstrated here, but the technique also works with minor adjustments when the opponent is using the De La Riva guard or the open guard. The key to this technique is to control the foot and the hip by holding the belt and blocking the opposite leg with your shoulder so your opponent can't close the leg over the foot for the counter.

1 John is in Jean Jacques's guard. He has managed to pin Jean Jacques's legs and is starting to pass. He holds Jean Jacques's belt with his right arm stiff to control the hips while his left hand holds Jean Jacques's right gi pants at the knee. Jean Jacques traps John's right leg by locking his left leg over it, blocking John from moving to his right.

2 John lowers his torso, reaches between his legs with his left hand, and grabs Jean Jacques's left foot, pulling it against his right thigh. At the same time, he puts his right elbow on Jean Jacques' left thigh while still holding the belt, thereby locking Jean Jacques's leg between his right elbow, the mat, and his right thigh. Should he fail to secure the leg, Jean Jacques would be free to move his hips to his own left, avoiding the leg lock and even moving to John's back.

NIQUES FIGHTING TECHNIQUES FIGHTING TECHNIQUES FIGHTING TECHNI
ING TECHNIQUES FIGHTING TECHNIQUES FIGHTING TECHNIQUES FIGHTIN
ES FIGHTING TECHNIQUES FIGHTING TECHNIQUES FIGHTING TECHNIQUES
TECHNIQUES FIGHTING TECHNIQUES FIGHTING TECHNIQUES FIGHTING TE
GHTIN QUES FIGHTING TECHNIQUES FIGH
IQUES G TECHNIQUES FIGHTING TECHNIQ

3 While still holding Jean Jacques's foot with his left hand and the belt with his right, John puts his weight on the right hand and uses it to pivot his body as he throws his left leg back. Notice that John's right leg is now sliding up under Jean Jacques's left leg. John needs to have his hips past Jean Jacques's knee before he goes for the submission.

4 Having passed his hips over the knee, John sits on the mat and pulls Jean Jacques's leg with his left hand. Notice John's leg position: his right leg is over Jean Jacques's leg with the knee bent, cradling the leg, and his left leg, foot back and knee bent, is pushing on the top of Jean Jacques's left thigh, cinching the noose tight. John is still holding Jean Jacques's belt with his right arm and pushing it toward the ground to keep the hips pinned.

5 John slides his left foot clockwise, crosses it under his right one, closes his thighs around Jean Jacques's left leg, and pulls on the heel and calf with both hands for the knee bar. The pressure on the knee is tremendous, and the submission is inevitable.

TING TECHNIQUES FIGHTING TECHNIQUES FIGHTING TECHNIQUES FIGHTI
UES FIGHTING TECHNIQUES FIGHTING TECHNIQUES FIGHTING TECHNIQUE
TECHNIQUES FIGHTING TECHNIQUES FIGHTING TECHNIQUES FIGHTING TE
FIGHTING TECHNIQUES FIGHTING TECHNIQUES FIGHTING TECHNIQUES FI
NIQUES FIGHTING TECHNIQUES FIGHTING TECHNIQUES FIGHTING TECHNI
ING TECHNIQUES FIGHTING TECHNIQUES FIGHTING TECHNIQUES FIGHTIN

48
Guard pass submission option 2: loop choke

Often the best option when trying to pass someone's guard is to go for a quick sub-mission. Jean Jacques is a firm believer in going for a footlock, a knee bar or even a choke if the opportunity arises. In this case, the opportunity presented is ripe for the loop choke because John sat up to defend the guard pass and has his head upright. The loop choke is a very powerful and surprising choke that will end any match in a submission when applied correctly.

1 Jean Jacques is standing as he attempts to pass John's guard. John is sitting up to defend the pass. Jean Jacques has his right hand on John's right collar near the chest, and his left hand grips John's right sleeve. When trying for the loop choke, it is very impor-tant not to hold the opponent's collar too high for two reasons: 1) he will realize the threat to his neck, and 2) the higher you grab the collar, the harder it will be to apply the choke because your hand and the collar will hit the side of your opponent's face.

2 Jean Jacques takes a short step to his left with his left foot as he attempts to pass the guard and get closer to John. John sits further forward as he extends his right arm to block Jean Jacques's left knee, stopping him from coming around for the pass. Jean Jacques's right hand opens up John's collar by pulling it lightly away. Subtlety is a must here to pre-vent your opponent from sensing the danger and defending.

3 Jean Jacques drops his body and loops John's collar under his chin, making sure that his right elbow passes over John's head.

FIGHTING TECHNIQUES FIGHTING TECHNIQUES FIGHTING TECHNI
NIQUES FIGHTING TECHNIQUES FIGHTING TECHNIQUES FIGHTING TECHNI
ING TECHNIQUES FIGHTING TECHNIQUES FIGHTING TECHNIQUES FIGHTIN
ES FIGHTING TECHNIQUES FIGHTING TECHNIQUES FIGHTING TECHNIQUES
TECHNIQUES FIGHTING TECHNIQUES FIGHTING TECHNIQUES FIGHTING TI
GHTIN ES FIGH
IQUES ECHNIQ

4 Jean Jacques lets go of John's right sleeve, wraps his left arm around John's right arm, and drops his chest to John's back, preventing him from pulling his head out of the loop.

5 Jean Jacques bends his left leg and drives his head down between John's right arm and thigh while pulling the collar tight with his right arm. It is very important not to let go of the grip on John's right arm; otherwise, he can spin out of the choke by turning to his own left.

6 Jean Jacques kneels down on his left knee and continues to roll over his left shoulder, still driving his head.

7 Jean Jacques continues to roll over his shoulder. He pulls John's collar tight around the neck and holds the right arm at all times to prevent John from escaping the pressure by turning to his left. Notice that Jean Jacques uses a motion similar to the one in drill 8, the side roll.

8 Jean Jacques continues to roll until he is across-side on John. His right arm holds John's right arm, and his left arm has tightened the collar around John's neck so much that John has no option but to submit or pass out.

139

FIGHTING TECHNIQUES FIGHTING TECHNIQUES FIGHTING TECHNIQUES FIGHTING TECHN
ING TECHNIQUES FIGHTING TECHNIQUES FIGHTING TECHNIQUES FIGHTING TECHNIQUES FIGHTI
ES FIGHTING TECHNIQUES FIGHTING TECHNIQUES FIGHTING TECHNIQUES FIGHTING TECHNIQUE
FIGHTING TECHNIQUES FIGHTING TECHNIQUES FIGHTING TECHNIQUES FIGHTING TE
FIGHTING TECHNIQUES FIGHTING TECHNIQUES FIGHTING TECHNIQUES FI
NIQUES FIGHTING TECHNIQUES FIGHTING TECHNIQUES FIGHTING TECHNI
NG TECHNIQUES FIGHTING TECHNIQUES FIGHTING TECHNIQUES FIGHTIN
G TECHNIQUES FIGHTING TECHNIQUES FIGHTING TECHNIQUES FIGHTIN

49
Guard pass counter 1: triangle choke

Allowing your opponent to pass your guard puts you at a great disadvantage in Brazilian jiu-jitsu, especially in competition where each point is fought with tenacity and the time constraints make a 3-point disadvantage large. Serious competitors must be able to anticipate guard pass variations and counter them decisively. In this section, we demonstrate a range of counters that will put you in the dominant position.

   A very effective and comtemporary method of passing the guard is to underhook one arm inside the opponent's arm and push the opposite leg down and pass over that side. The underhook keeps the opponent's shoulder flat on the ground, giving the passer significant control. Here Jean Jacques presents a very simple and equally effective counter. However, you must start the counter immediately after the underhook; otherwise, the passer will gain too much control over your torso for the technique to work.

1 John attempts to pass Jean Jacques's guard with the underhook. His left arm is underhooked around Jean Jacques's right arm near the armpit, and his right hand pushes down on Jean Jacques's left leg as he steps over it. Jean Jacques immediately pushes off John's shoulders with both hands to prevent him from driving his body forward and on top of Jean Jacques's torso.

2 Jean Jacques releases his left foot from under John's body, kicks his foot out and up, and slides his torso toward the right by pushing off his right leg. John fights to control Jean Jacques's left leg by gripping Jean Jacques's left ankle with his right hand and trying to push the leg down to resume the pass. John also wants to make sure Jean Jacques doesn't close his legs around the back for full guard.

3 Jean Jacques loops his right leg over John's back as he turns his upper body toward the right. John still tries to push and control Jean Jacques's left leg in his attempt to pass.

4 Jean Jacques hooks his right foot under John's right arm and pushes John's left shoulder down and away.

5 He then loops his left leg around John's head. John cannot simply stand up because his arms are locked by Jean Jacques's right leg and arm, and Jean Jacques's left leg presses down on John's right shoulder.

6 Jean Jacques drives John's left arm across his chest. At this point, Jean Jacques has so much control over John's upper body that he can release his right foot hook.

7 Jean Jacques holds his left shin with his right hand to lock the position, then locks his right leg over his left foot for the figure-four around the neck and arm for the triangle choke.

FIGHTING TECHNIQUES FIGHTING TECHNIQUES FIGHTING TECHNIQUES FIGHTING TECHN
TING TECHNIQUES FIGHTING TECHNIQUES FIGHTING TECHNIQUES FIGHTI
UES FIGHTING TECHNIQUES FIGHTING TECHNIQUES FIGHTING TECHNIQUE
TECHNIQUES FIGHTING TECHNIQUES FIGHTING TECHNIQUES FIGHTING TE
FIGHTING TECHNIQUES FIGHTING TECHNIQUES FIGHTING TECHNIQUES FI
NIQUES FIGHTING TECHNIQUES FIGHTING TECHNIQUES FIGHTING TECHNI
NG TECHNIQUES FIGHTING TECHNIQUES FIGHTING TECHNIQUES FIGHTIN

50

Guard pass counter 1 (variation): shoulder lock

In this variation on the previous technique, John is passing with the under-hook, and Jean Jacques counters. Here, however, when Jean Jacques locks John's right arm with his right foot hook, John reacts by planting his right foot and tries to drive his body forward in an effort to escape and release his arm. Jean Jacques reviews the possibilities and opts for a painful shoulder lock. We pick up at the point when John's arm is hooked by Jean Jacques's foot (step 49.4).

1 Jean Jacques has hooked John's right arm with his right foot. John plants his right foot on the mat, pushes off it, and drives his body forward, trying to release his arm.

2 Jean Jacques pushes John's head with his right arm, stopping John's forward motion and forcing him away. Jean Jacques slides his torso to his own right and loops his left leg over John's head.

NIQUES FIGHTING TECHNIQUES FIGHTING TECHNIQUES FIGHTING TECHNIQUES FIGHTING TECHNI
ING TECHNIQUES FIGHTING TECHNIQUES FIGHTING TECHNIQUES FIGHTING TECHNIQUES FIGHTIN
ES FIGHTING TECHNIQUES FIGHTING TECHNIQUES FIGHTING TECHNIQUES FIGHTING TECHNIQUES
TECHNIQUES FIGHTING TECHNIQUES FIGHTING TECHNIQUES FIGHTING TECHNIQUES FIGHTING TI
GHTING TECH   HNIQUES FIGH
IQUES FIGHT   TING TECHNIQ

3 Jean Jacques pushes down on the left leg, forcing John's head to the mat, then sits up and reaches with his right arm to grab John's right arm.

4 With his right hand, Jean Jacques grabs John's right sleeve near the wrist and pulls it toward his own head. He assists the move by using his left hand to grab John's sleeve at the elbow and leans back, pulling the arm to the mat for a painful shoulder lock.

TING TECHNIQUES FIGHTING TECHNIQUES FIGHTING TECHNIQUES FIGHTING TECH
UES FIGHTING TECHNIQUES FIGHTING TECHNIQUES FIGHTING TECHNIQUES FIGHTI
TECHNIQUES FIGHTING TECHNIQUES FIGHTING TECHNIQUES FIGHTING TECHNIQUE
FIGHTING TECHNIQUES FIGHTING TECHNIQUES FIGHTING TECHNIQUES FIGHTING TE
NIQUES FIGHTING TECHNIQUES FIGHTING TECHNIQUES FIGHTING TECHNIQUES FI
ING TECHNIQUES FIGHTING TECHNIQUES FIGHTING TECHNIQUES FIGHTING TECHNI
TECHNIQUES FIGHTIN

51
Guard pass counter 1 (variation): armlock with strong opponent

In another variation on position 49, when Jean Jacques hooks his right leg around John's arm, John reacts by closing his arm. Assuming that John is a very strong opponent, Jean Jacques will not be able to pull the right arm for the shoulder lock. In that case, Jean Jacques will use John's strength and momentum against him. We pick up the technique at the point where Jean Jacques hooks his leg around John's arm (step 49.4)

1 Jean Jacques has hooked John's right arm with his right foot. John is a very strong fighter and keeps his arm closed, making it difficult for Jean Jacques to pull his arm open.

2 John braces off his right foot and pushes his body forward onto Jean Jacques. Jean Jacques uses John's momentum, plants his left foot on the mat, and pushes off it, lifting his hips off the mat and sliding his body to his left.

2 Reverse Angle Jean Jacques hooks John's right arm with his right leg. Notice that Jean Jacques has placed his left foot on John's right hip.

3 With his left foot on John's right hip, Jean Jacques pushes him back toward the mat, rolling him over. Because John was already pushing his weight over Jean Jacques, the fall occurs easily.

NIQUES FIGHTING TECHNIQUES FIGHTING TECHNIQUES FIGHTING TECHN
ING TECHNIQUES FIGHTING TECHNIQUES FIGHTING TECHNIQUES FIGHTIN
ES FIGHTING TECHNIQUES FIGHTING TECHNIQUES FIGHTING TECHNIQUES
TECHNIQUES FIGHTING TECHNIQUES FIGHTING TECHNIQUES FIGHTING TI
GHTING TECHNIQUES FIGHTING TECHNIQUES FIGHTING TECHNIQUES FIGH
IQUES FIGHTING TECHNIQUES FIGHTING TECHNIQUES FIGHTING TECHNI

4 As John's back hits the mat, Jean Jacques releases John's left arm from his right armpit and lassoes the same arm with his own left arm.

5 Jean Jacques loops his left leg over John's head. Notice that throughout this whole sequence Jean Jacques's right leg has remained hooked on John's right arm; otherwise, John would just come back up. At this point, Jean Jacques can release the hook.

6 Jean Jacques releases his right foot from John's right arm, plants the right foot on the mat, and pushes off it to help turn his torso toward John's right leg—a move that is necessary for achieving the proper angle for the armlock.

7 Jean Jacques locks his right leg over John's head and lifts his hips as he pulls on John's left arm with both hands, applying pressure to the elbow joint for the armlock. Again, it is important for Jean Jacques's hips to be past John's elbow; otherwise, the armlock won't work because the pressure would not be on the joint, and it would be too easy for John to slide his elbow past Jean Jacques's hips (a standard defense against the armlock).

52

Guard pass counter 2: sweep

A competitor trying to pass your guard will often do so by committing his weight so much that you can reverse him. The key to these reversals is to sense your opponent's weight and make sure you block and control his arm so he can't open it and block the reversal.

1 John has his right arm around Jean Jacques's left leg as he attempts to pass the guard to that side. He may be trying to grab Jean Jacques's left ankle for greater control to assist the pass. Jean Jacques uses his left hand to grab and control John's right wrist, making sure it stays tucked in.

2 Jean Jacques sits up, reaches over John's right shoulder, and grabs John's belt with his right hand. To ensure that the sweep works, Jean Jacques must grab the belt over the shoulder on the same side that John is attempting to pass.

3 Jean Jacques baits John to pass, allowing him to throw his weight over his right shoulder as he commits himself to get to Jean Jacques's left side. John pushes off his extended left leg as he drives his right shoulder onto Jean Jacques to keep him pinned. Jean Jacques continues pushing John's right arm in and rotates his head as if he wanted to get under John's belly. Notice that he may or may not end up with his left leg trapping John's left leg (it depends on the particulars of the situation); the sweep will work regardless.

4 Jean Jacques continues to rotate under John, still pushing John's arm in, and pulls on John's belt with his left arm. At this point, John is completely off balance to his own right and cannot use his arm to block the reversal.

5 With John's entire weight on top of him and his body twisted, Jean Jacques continues to turn under John and executes the reversal as he pulls the belt with his right arm and pushes John's right arm in with his own left arm.

6 Jean Jacques ends up on top of John, either on the half-guard, as in this case, or across-side if his leg doesn't hook inside John's legs.

53

Guard pass counter 3: sweep (opponent passing with underhooks)

John is attempting to pass with underhooks (both hands under the arms). In this case, John has both arms under Jean Jacques's legs and holds his belt. This is another very common, effective, and safe guard pass because the position of John's arms (under Jean Jacques's legs) prevents both the triangle and the armlock counters. If Jean Jacques doesn't react, John will lift his hips, roll, and stack Jean Jacques over his shoulder with full control of the hips and the luxury to pass the guard on either side.

1 John is attempting to pass Jean Jacques's guard with both arms under the legs and a firm grip on the belt. Jean Jacques holds John's wrists with his hands and uses the grip to push his hips away from John to keep him from stacking.

2 Jean Jacques hooks his left foot under John's right leg while still holding the right wrist.

3 Jean Jacques opens his right leg, plants his foot on the mat, and sits up, bracing on his left elbow and reaching with his right arm over John's back. At the same time, Jean Jacques slides his left leg across John's hips until he hooks his left foot outside of John's left hip.

3 Reverse Angle (detail) Notice Jean Jacques's left leg in front of John's hips and his foot hooked outside of John's left hip.

FIGHTING TECHNIQUES FIGHTING TECHNIQUES FIGHTING TECHNIQUES FIGHTING TECHN
ING TECHNIQUES FIGHTING TECHNIQUES FIGHTING TECHNIQUES FIGHTIN
ES FIGHTING TECHNIQUES FIGHTING TECHNIQUES FIGHTING TECHNIQUES
TECHNIQUES FIGHTING TECHNIQUES FIGHTING TECHNIQUES FIGHTING TI
GHTIN
NIQUES

4 Jean Jacques grips John's belt as he lies on his left side.

5 Jean Jacques rolls over his shoulder, throwing his right leg over John's head, and pulls John's belt with his right hand.

6 As he continues to roll over his back, Jean Jacques pulls John's right arm away from him, forcing his body to turn to the right. At this point, John has no brace to his right and begins to fall backwards.

7 Jean Jacques continues to turn over, forcing John's back to hit the mat.

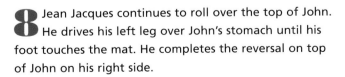

8 Jean Jacques continues to roll over the top of John. He drives his left leg over John's stomach until his foot touches the mat. He completes the reversal on top of John on his right side.

FIGHTING TECHNIQUES FIGHTING TECHNIQUES FIGHTING TECHNIQUES FIGHTI
ES FIGHTING TECHNIQUES FIGHTING TECHNIQUES FIGHTING TECHNIQUE
TECHNI FIGHTING TECHNIQUES FIGHTING TECHNIQUES FIGHTING TE
FIGHTING TECHNIQUES FIGHTING TECHNIQUES FIGHTING TECHNIQUES FIG
IQUES FIGHTING TECHNIQUES FIGHTING TECHNIQUES FIGHTING TECHNI
NG TECHNIQUES FIGHTING TECHNIQUES FIGHTING TECHNIQUES FIGHTING

54

Guard pass counter 4: armlock

The traditional one-arm-under method of passing the guard is very solid and precise. Your one arm under the leg grabs the belt and controls the opponent's hips, keeping him from moving away from you. You have the option of passing to that side and around the leg by stacking the opponent on his head, or should he block that side, you can simply pass to the inside as you slide your knee over his other leg, which is down on the mat. Here, Jean Jacques demonstrates a very effective way to counter this pass technique and goes one step further to the armlock.

1 John attempts to pass Jean Jacques's guard. His left arm is around Jean Jacques's right leg, and his hand grabs Jean Jacques's belt, keeping Jean Jacques from backing away to create space. His right arm controls Jean Jacques's gi, and he could use the right hand to push Jean Jacques's left leg down and pass over it. However, Jean Jacques immediately takes hold of John's left wrist with his right hand and blocks John's right arm with his left hand on the elbow.

2 Before John can pull him back and stack him, Jean Jacques opens his right leg and plants his foot on the mat, using it to escape his hips to the right as he pushes John's head away with his right arm, creating space.

3 Jean Jacques continues pushing John's head down to the mat, sits up, and plants his left elbow on the mat.

FIGHTING TECHNIQUES FIGHTING TECHNIQUES FIGHTING TECHNIQUES FIG
NIQUES FIGHTING TECHNIQUES FIGHTING TECHNIQUES FIGHTING TECHN
ING TECHNIQUES FIGHTING TECHNIQUES FIGHTING TECHNIQUES FIGHTIN
ES FIGHTING TECHNIQUES FIGHTING TECHNIQUES FIGHTING TECHNIQUES
TECHNIQUES FIGHTING TECHNIQUES FIGHTING TECHNIQUES FIGHTING TI
GHTIN   ES FIGH
IQUE   TECHNIC

4 Jean Jacques comes up off his left arm and pushes off it as he kicks his right leg over John's back. Notice that Jean Jacques loops his right arm, readying it to grab an arm or a gi.

5 Jean Jacques ends up on John's back. His right hand grabs around John's right arm, setting up the armlock, and his left leg is hooked inside John's left arm. Jean Jacques now locks his right foot hook on John's right leg. At this point, Jean Jacques can fight to take the back control and place his left foot hook on John's left hip or, should John resist and try holding the leg with his arm, Jean Jacques follows up with the technique shown here.

6 Jean Jacques continues his rotation in a counterclockwise direction as he rolls over his right shoulder and kicks his left leg up, forcing John to follow because the leg traps John's left arm. Should John resist, he will break his shoulder.

7 As he finishes the rotation, Jean Jacques has the armlock: his arms control John's right arm, his left leg traps John's left arm, and his right leg is over John's hips.

8 All Jean Jacques has to do is lift his hips and pull John's arm toward his chest for the armlock.

FIGHTING TECHNIQUES FIGHTING TECHNIQUES

55
Bear hug guard pass counter

Bear hugging your opponent's legs is a very effective technique for passing the guard. By trapping the legs and pushing them together, not only do you deter his blocks and hooks, but you also restrict his hips. Once you bear hug the legs, you slowly move your body around them to one side and push your shoulders forward into your opponent until you get to his side. Jean Jacques here demonstrates one of his favorite counters to the bear hug pass. His opponent's commitment to holding the legs together against him means he has no arms free to block the reversal.

1 John is attempting to pass Jean Jacques's guard by bear hugging the legs. He has both arms around Jean Jacques's legs, bringing them together and flat on the mat. John is circling to his own right to get across-side, and he drives his right shoulder into Jean Jacques. Jean Jacques knows that he has to counter immediately or John will achieve the across-side position. The first thing he does is sit up and take his back off the mat; otherwise, he would have very few options to defend. His left hand grabs and blocks the outside of John's right elbow, momentarily stopping his advance.

2 Jean Jacques leans forward and bear hugs John's back. He tightens his arms around John's chest, preferably locking his hands.

3 As John puts his weight on the right shoulder and moves forward, Jean Jacques uses that commitment against him. Since his arms are locked, John cannot open them to block the reversal. Jean Jacques lies back toward his left and kicks his legs up, twisting John's trunk in a clockwise direction by pulling down with his right arm and pushing up with his left.

FIGHTING TECHNIQUES FIGHTING TECHNIQUES FIGHTING TECHNIQUES FIG
NIQUES FIGHTING TECHNIQUES FIGHTING TECHNIQUES FIGHTING TECHNI
ING TECHNIQUES FIGHTING TECHNIQUES FIGHTING TECHNIQUES FIGHTIN
ES FIGHTING TECHNIQUES FIGHTING TECHNIQUES FIGHTING TECHNIQUES
TECHNIQUES FIGHTING TECHNIQUES FIGHTING TECHNIQUES FIGHTING TE
GHTIN   S FIGH
IQUES   TECHNIC
G TI   TING

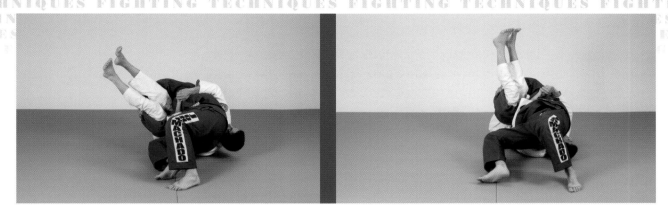

4 Jean Jacques continues rolling and pulling John over the top of him. Notice how Jean Jacques's hands are locked around John's chest, keeping his body tight against John's. This is very important, as any space between the two will allow John to twist back and gain side control.

5 Jean Jacques continues to swing his body to his right as he brings John over with him. Notice how Jean Jacques uses his legs to add the momentum to the motion by swinging them up and over. Had he kept his legs straight, he would have had to rely on arm strength alone to bring down John. Swinging his legs gives him much more leverage and momentum to accomplish the roll.

6 Jean Jacques ends up on John's left side on the top.

7 Jean Jacques adjusts his side-control position with his right arm under John's neck and drives his left shoulder forward, pushing John's right shoulder back to flatten him out. Notice that Jean Jacques's left hand is next to John's left hip, preventing him from sliding his left leg in to replace the guard.

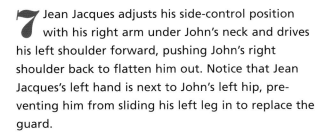

56

Stacking guard pass counter: sweep to armlock

The very effective stacking guard pass is used widely in tournaments. A serious competitor should know both the pass and how to counter it. Here, Jean Jacques demonstrates his favorite counter to the stack, resulting in a sweep and a submission. The key to this defense, like most moves, is to be able to react quickly and apply the hook.

1 John is attempting to pass Jean Jacques's guard using the stacking method. His left hand holds Jean Jacques's left collar close to his neck, and his right hand holds Jean Jacques's belt or his gi pants near the buttocks to prevent him from rolling over his shoulder as he gets stacked.

2 John pushes off his feet and lifts Jean Jacques's hips off the mat, decreasing both his mobility and power. John puts his weight forward as he stacks Jean Jacques's legs and hips over his head. He pulls himself by his left arm, applying even more pressure on Jean Jacques. Notice that John uses his left shoulder to help drive Jean Jacques's right leg over the head. If Jean Jacques doesn't react at this point, John will pass his guard. His first move is to put his right hand on John's left hip to block him and create the space to lower his hips.

FIGHTING TECHNIQUES FIGHTING TECHNIQUES FIGHTING TECHNIQUES FIGHTING TECHNI NIQUES FIGHTING TECHNIQUES FIGHTING TECHNIQUES FIGHTING TECHNIQUES FIGHTING TECHNI ING TECHNIQUES FIGHTING TECHNIQUES FIGHTING TECHNIQUES FIGHTING TECHNIQUES FIGHTIN ES FIGHTING TECHNIQUES FIGHTING TECHNIQUES FIGHTING TECHNIQUES FIGHTING TECHNIQUES TECHNIQUES FIGHTING TECHNIQUES FIGHTING TECHNIQUES FIGHTING TECHNIQUES FIGHTING TI GHTING TECHNIQUES FIGHTING TECHNIQUES FIGHTING TECHNIQUES FIGHTING TECHNIQUES FIGH IQUES FIGHTING TECHNIQUES FIGHTING TECHNIQUES FIGHTING TECHNIQUES FIGHTING TECHNIQUE

3 Jean Jacques drops his left leg, hooks his foot under John's right leg, and grabs John's left elbow with his right hand.

4 Pulling off that hook, Jean Jacques spins his body to his left. At the same time, he opens John's left elbow toward his head to allow his right leg the freedom it needs to drop the hips down. Jean Jacques hooks his left arm inside John's right leg. Notice that Jean Jacques's right hand controls John's left elbow.

5 Jean Jacques kicks his legs toward his right (clockwise motion), pulls John's left arm with his right arm, and lifts the right leg with his left arm, destroying John's base. His right leg pushes on John's left arm, and his left leg pushes John's right leg, forcing him to fall.

6 Jean Jacques uses John's fall to help himself come over the top. At this point, he lets go of John's right leg and reaches around John's right arm with his left arm, grabbing the elbow.

7 Jean Jacques pulls John's elbow up until his wrist locks over his own shoulder. Jean Jacques traps the wrist with his shoulder and head and applies pressure to the elbow with both hands, pulling it down for the armlock.

8 Should John be able to spin his wrist and defend the armlock, Jean Jacques will fall to his right and extend his right leg until his knee is past John's neck. Notice that Jean Jacques's left leg is already in perfect position for a triangle, and John's right arm is inside—also in perfect position for the lock.

FIGHTING TECHNIQUES FIGHTING TECHNIQUES FIGHTING TECHNIQUES FIGHTING TE
NIQUES FIGHTING TECHNIQUES FIGHTING TECHNIQUES FIGHTING TECHN
ING TECHNIQUES FIGHTING TECHNIQUES FIGHTING TECHNIQUES FIGHTIN
ES FIGHTING TECHNIQUES FIGHTING TECHNIQUES FIGHTING TECHNIQUES
TECHNIQUES FIGHTING TECHNIQUES FIGHTING TECHNIQUES FIGHTING T
HTING TECHNIQUES FIGHTING TECHNIQUES FIGHTING TECHNIQUES FIG
IQUES FIGHTING TECHNIQUES FIGHTING TECHNIQUES FIGHTING TECHNI

9 Jean Jacques drives his right leg counterclockwise, forcing John to his left. Notice Jean Jacques is still holding John's right arm to prevent him from pulling it back and removing it from the imminent triangle.

10 Jean Jacques pulls John's right arm across his body all the way to the right . . .

11 And locks the figure-four with his left leg over the right foot for the triangle. He applies the pressure by pulling John's head with both hands as he closes the gap between his legs for the choke.

57

toreana guard pass counter: standing up

Allowing your opponent to pass your guard is a big no-no in Brazilian jiu-jitsu, especially in competition. When you are behind in points or you have been slow to react to a move, it is sometimes better to stand up and start over than to allow the opponent to reach your side. Here, Jean Jacques was late in his defense, so he has to resort to a stand-up counter because John already has full control of both legs, which are pinned to the mat. The technique that Jean Jacques demonstrates here is an effective general counter to the toreana guard pass.

1 Jean Jacques is in the butterfly guard with John attempting to pass. John has both hands on Jean Jacques's knees and has control of them as he pins the legs to the mat. Should Jean Jacques not react quickly, John will reach side control simply by running to one side or the other while keeping his body weight on Jean Jacques's legs.

FIGHTING TECHNIQUES FIGHTING TECHNIQUES FIGHTING TECHNIQUES FIGHTING TECHNIQUES FIGHTING TECHN ING TECHNIQUES FIGHTING TECHNIQUES FIGHTING TECHNIQUES FIGHTING TECHNIQUES FIGHTIN ES FIGHTING TECHNIQUES FIGHTING TECHNIQUES FIGHTING TECHNIQUES FIGHTING TECHNIQUES TECHNIQUES FIGHTING TECHNIQUES FIGHTING TECHNIQUES FIGHTING TECHNIQUES FIGHTING TI GHTING TECHNIQUES FIGHTING TECHNIQUES FIGHTING TECHNIQUES FIGHTING TECHNIQUES FIGH IQUES FIGHTING TECHNIQUES FIGHTING TECHNIQUES FIGHTING TECHNIQUES FIGHTING TECHNIQ

2 Jean Jacques turns his body to his left, grabs John's belt with his right hand, and stiffens his arm. At the same time, Jean Jacques plants his left hand on the mat slightly behind his left hip.

3 Jean Jacques stands up in base (see drill 1, standing up in base), except that he uses his right arm to help push off John. He pushes off his left hand and right foot to prop his body up and brings his left leg back through the bridge formed by his bracing leg and arm. At the same time, Jean Jacques keeps his right arm stiff, pushing John away and down to prevent him from following.

FIGHTING TECHNIQUES FIGHTING TECHNIQUES FIGHTING TECHNIQUES FIGHTING TECHN TING TECHNIQUES FIGHTING TECHNIQUES FIGHTING TECHNIQUES FIGHTI ES FIGHTING TECHNIQUES FIGHTING TECHNIQUES FIGHTING TECHNIQUE TECHNI FIGHTING TECHNIQUES FIGHTING TECHNIQUES FIGHTING TE FIGHTING TECHNIQUES FIGHTING TECHNIQUES FIGHTING TECHNIQUES FIG NIQUES FIGHTING TECHNIQUES FIGHTING TECHNIC ING TECHNIQUES FIGHTING TECHNIQUES FIGHTING

58
Reversal from the butterfly guard 1: helicopter sweep

The ability to reverse an opponent from the guard or the half-guard cannot be overestimated in Brazilian jiu-jitsu. In competition, you achieve 2 points for the reversal, but more important, the reversal brings you on top and in a better position to score more points. While it is true that in BJJ the athlete on the bottom has many resources with which to defend himself and even submit his opponent, the sport and real-life fighting offer greater rewards for those on top. In this case, Jean Jacques is using a movement similar to the one demonstrated in the side-roll drill (drill 8) to pull off the reversal.

2 As John begins to pass, he plants his left foot on the mat and steps forward with his left leg. Jean Jacques pushes off his right foot and starts rotating his body toward his left, pushing John's right hand into his body to keep him from bracing.

1 John is attempting to pass Jean Jacques's sitting guard (butterfly guard or guard with hooks). John has already achieved a slight advantage, and he has his left knee inside Jean Jacques's hooks, forcing Jean Jacques to escape his hips back and disengage his hook. Jean Jacques intercepts and grabs John's right wrist to prevent him from grabbing Jean Jacques's left leg. From here, John can go for a variety of guard passes, such as the toreana or the knee-across technique. Jean Jacques has his right hand inside John's right collar, and his left hand intercepts and controls John's right hand, preventing him from grabbing either his gi pants or collar for the pass.

3 Jean Jacques continues to roll to his left. His left leg extends inside John's legs while he pulls on the collar with his right hand.

4 Once his back hits the mat, Jean Jacques's body is perpendicular to John's. His right hand continues to pull John's torso over, and his left hand continues to push John's right hand in. His left leg is now solidly hooked inside John's left leg and will help bring him over the top.

5 Jean Jacques continues the reversal as he rolls over his back and kicks his left leg across his body to the right, catapulting John over his own right shoulder.

6 Jean Jacques continues to roll to his right. Note that he still controls John's right gi sleeve and collar. He actually uses them to help reverse John by pulling them in a circular motion.

7 Jean Jacques continues to roll over his shoulders . . .

8 Until he lands on top of John on the opposite side for the 2-point reversal.

FIGHTING TECHNIQUES FIGHTING TECHNIQUES FIGHTING TECHNIQUES FIGHTING TECHN
TING TECHNIQUES FIGHTING TECHNIQUES FIGHTING TECHNIQUES FIGHTI
UES FIGHTING TECHNIQUES FIGHTING TECHNIQUES FIGHTING TECHNIQUE
CHNIQUES FIGHTING TECHNIQUES FIGHTING TECHNIQUES FIGHTING TE
IGHTING TECHNIQUES FIGHTING TECHNIQUES FIGHTING TECHNIQUES FIG
IQUES FIGHTING TECHNIQUES FIGHTING TECHNIQUES FIGHTING TECHNI
TECHNIQUES FIGHTING TECHNIQUES FIGHTING TECHNIQUES FIGHTING

59

Reversal from the butterfly guard 2

Jean Jacques here demonstrates a second technique for reversing an opponent from the butterfly guard. Jean Jacques starts by obtaining inside control (with his arms inside Todd's arms) and tries for an overhead sweep. If Todd successfully defends, as demonstrated here, then Jean Jacques will go for the second part of the move and reverse by going forward. Jean Jacques fully intends to use the overhead sweep, and it is only after Todd's proper defense that he will pursue his second option. In using these combinations, you should always try to succeed in the first part; otherwise, your opponent will sense your half-hearted effort and may actually advance his position.

1 Jean Jacques has Todd in his butterfly guard, and both his feet are hooked inside Todd's thighs. He also has achieved inside control with his arms inside Todd's arms, his hands clasped, and his torso tight against Todd's chest. Notice that Jean Jacques is sitting up with his back off the mat. A very common mistake in executing the butterfly guard is to have your back on the mat, which eliminates many of the options available from this position.

2 Jean Jacques rocks backwards, slides his arms up onto Todd's back until they are under the armpits, and brings Todd over him.

3 Jean Jacques kicks his legs up, trying to sweep Todd over his head. At this point, Todd wisely opens his arms and braces forward to block the overhead sweep.

FIGHTING TECHNIQUES FIGHTING TECHNIQUES FIGHTING TECHNIQUES FIGHTING TECHNIQUES FIGHTING TECHNIQUES FIGHTING TECHNIQUES FIGHTING TECHNIQUES FIGHTING TECHNIQUES FIGHTING TECHNIQUES FIGHTING TECHNIQUES FIGHTING TECHNIQUES FIGHTING TECHNIQUES FIGHTING TECHNIQUES FIGHTING TECHNIQUES FIGHTING TECHNIQUES FIGHTING TECHNIQUES FIGHTING TECHNIQUES FIGHTING TECHNIQUES FIGHTING TECHNIQUES FIGHTING TECHNIQUES

4 Once he realizes his overhead sweep has been properly defended, Jean Jacques rocks forward and slides his arms down, still keeping his torso tight against Todd's chest. Todd relaxes, assuming that the danger is over and that they will simply return to the original position.

5 Using the momentum of his forward rock, Jean Jacques continues to sit up and slides his bear hug farther down to Todd's lower back. He plants his left foot on the mat just in front of Todd's left shin, pushes off his left leg to move his hips away from Todd's hips, and brings his right leg back until his foot touches his thigh. Notice Jean Jacques still bear hugs Todd tightly, as any space between them will greatly reduce the force necessary for the sweep.

6 Jean Jacques continues to press forward, driving Todd backward. Jean Jacques raises his hips off the mat and circles his right foot back. His head and chest push on Todd's chest while he pulls his bear hug on Todd's lower back, forcing him to fall back. Notice that Jean Jacques's left foot is blocking Todd's left shin. Jean Jacques continues to push forward until Todd's back is on the mat. Jean Jacques has used the same movement as in drill 3, coming up to your knee.

7 Just prior to Todd's back hitting the mat, Jean Jacques releases his grip, leaves his left arm under Todd's right armpit, braces his right hand on the mat, and drives his left knee across and over Todd's left thigh. Jean Jacques keeps his toes on the mat to block Todd's left shin, which keeps Todd from pulling half-guard.

8 Jean Jacques continues to drive forward for the guard pass.

TING TECHNIQUES FIGHTING TECHNIQUES FIGHTING TECHNIQUES FIGHTING TECHN
UES FIGHTING TECHNIQUES FIGHTING TECHNIQUES FIGHTING TECHNIQUES FIGHTI
TECHNIQUES FIGHTING TECHNIQUES FIGHTING TECHNIQUES FIGHTING TECHNIQUE
FIGHTING TECHNIQUES FIGHTING TECHNIQUES FIGHTING TECHNIQUES FIGHTING TE
FIGHTING TECHNIQUES FIGHTING TECHNIQUES FIGHTING TECHNIQUES FIGHTING TE
NIQUES FIGHTING TECHNIQUES FIGHTING TECHNIQUES FIGHTING TECHNI
ING TECHNIQUES FIGHTING TECHNIQUES FIGHTING TECHNIQUES FIGHTING

60

Reversal from the butterfly guard 3 (opponent defends)

Jean Jacques here tries to use a hook sweep to reverse John, but John
defends it properly by pushing off his arms and putting his weight back.
Jean Jacques takes advantage of the defense and counters with another
reversal. Notice that he again uses the movement found in drill 3.

1 Jean Jacques has John in his butterfly guard with
hooks inside. His right hand grabs onto John's left
gi pants by the knee, and his left hand controls the right
collar, setting up the hook sweep to John's right side.

2 Jean Jacques escapes his hips to the right
as he pulls John toward him by the collar
and the leg.

3 John defends the sweep well, quickly
pushing off his arms and sitting back on
his heels to keep his weight back.

FIGHTING TECHNIQUES FIGHTING TECHNIQUES FIGHTING TECHNIQUES FIGHTING
NIQUES FIGHTING TECHNIQUES FIGHTING TECHNIQUES FIGHTING TECHNI
ING TECHNIQUES FIGHTING TECHNIQUES FIGHTING TECHNIQUES FIGHTIN
ES FIGHTING TECHNIQUES FIGHTING TECHNIQUES FIGHTING TECHNIQUES
TECHNIQUES FIGHTING TECHNIQUES FIGHTING TECHNIQUES FIGHTING TE
GHTING TECHNIQUES FIGHTING TECHNIQUES FIGHTING TECHNIQUES FIGH

4 Using the same motion as in drill 3, Jean Jacques tucks his right foot in and follows John's body forward, coming up on to him. Notice that Jean Jacques used his grip on the pants and collar to assist; also note Jean Jacques's left knee is ready to drive on John's chest.

5 Jean Jacques continues to rise off the ground and pushes forward on John's chest with his left arm and knee while pulling on John's left leg, forcing John to fall backward for the reversal.

6 Still gripping John's left leg, Jean Jacques pushes down on John's chest with his left hand, pinning him to the mat. With his right hand, Jean Jacques pushes John's left knee to the left and steps over it with his right leg, assuring himself of a great position for a guard pass of his own or for going directly for the mounted position.

TECHNIQUES FIGHTING TECHNIQUES FIGHTING TECHNIQUES FIGHTING TECHNIQUES FIGHTI
UES FIGHTING TECHNIQUES FIGHTING TECHNIQUES FIGHTING TECHNIQUE
TECHNIQUES FIGHTING TECHNIQUES FIGHTING TECHNIQUES FIGHTING TE
FIGHTING TECHNIQUES FIGHTING TECHNIQUES FIGHTING TECHNIQUES FI
NIQUES FIGHTING TECHNIQUES FIGHTING TECHNIQUES FIGHTING TECHNI
ING TECHNIQUES FIGHTING TECHNIQUES FIGHTING TECHNIQUES FIGHTIN

61

Reversal from the butterfly guard 4: sweep

This sweep from the butterfly guard is especially effective when the opponent has a tight grip on your collar and is posturing up, using his arm on your chest to keep distance.

1 Jean Jacques uses the butterfly guard against John's passing attempt. John has his left arm bracing against Jean Jacques's chest to keep distance.

2 Jean Jacques uses his left hand to give John's left gi collar to his right hand just under John's left triceps. Once he grabs the collar, Jean Jacques pulls it tight toward himself, locking John's left forearm against his chest. It is very important to pull the collar tight; otherwise, John will be able to pull his arm out. (In that case, you will use technique 62.)

FIGHTING TECHNIQUES FIGHTING

3 Jean Jacques plants his left hand on the mat and uses it to slide his hips to his left. Notice how Jean Jacques's hips are far to John's right side. This is very important, as he wants to roll John over his left side.

4 Jean Jacques grabs the back of John's right shoulder with his left hand and drops his right shoulder and knee toward the mat. He pulls John's body up and uses a twisting motion as if he were turning a wheel clockwise to force John to fall to Jean Jacques's right. It is very important for Jean Jacques to pull John over John's left shoulder rather than to pull him directly forward. This mistake ruins many a sweep attempt.

62

Reversal from the butterfly guard 5: sweep (opponent defends)

In this variation of technique 61, John reacts quickly to having his arm pinned and pulls it back. Jean Jacques takes advantage of John's reaction (leaning back) and goes forward for the sweep.

1 Jean Jacques begins the sweep much like technique 61. He uses John's lapel to trap John's left arm against his chest while his left hand controls John's right gi sleeve.

2 Sensing that his left arm is threatened, John reacts quickly and yanks his arm back as he leans back and sits on his heels.

3 Jean Jacques takes advantage of John's reaction and follows him, using John's momentum to pull himself forward. He tucks his right foot in, rocks forward on his right leg, and slides his arm between John's right arm and side of his body. Jean Jacques pushes off his left leg and puts his head on John's left side.

4 Jean Jacques uses his left shoulder on John's chest to continue to push him toward the mat, assisting the move by pushing off his left leg, forcing John to fall to John's left.

5 Jean Jacques continues to drive John to the mat with his shoulder. Notice the position of Jean Jacques's left hand gripping John's ribcage.

6 Jean Jacques ends up on top with the reversal.

TING TECHNIQUES FIGHTING TECHNIQUES FIGHTING TECHNIQUES FIGHTI
UES FIGHTING TECHNIQUES FIGHTING TECHNIQUES FIGHTING TECHNIQUE
TECHNI FIGHTING TECHNIQUES FIGHTING TECHNIQUES FIGHTING TE
FIGHTING TECHNIQUES FIGHTING TECHNIQUES FIGHTING TECHNIQUES FIG
NIQUES FIGHTING TECHNIQUES FIGHTING TECHNIQUES FIGHTING TECHNI
ING TECHNIQUES FIGHTING TECHNIQUES FIGHTING TECHNIQUES FIGHTING

63

Reversal from the butterfly guard 6: taking the back

Another extremely effective option to use from the butterfly guard is taking the back, which will score you 2 points for the reversal. The key to this move, like many other Brazilian jiu-jitsu moves, is to use the opponent's reaction to your benefit.

1 John is attempting to pass Jean Jacques's butterfly guard. He grips both legs with his hands and pins Jean Jacques's feet to the mat. If Jean Jacques doesn't react properly, John will quickly gain the side. All John needs to do is jump over to the left while keeping Jean Jacques's feet pressed against the mat. Jean Jacques holds John's left collar with his right hand and the right sleeve with his left hand.

2 Since John is applying his weight forward to press Jean Jacques's feet down on the mat, Jean Jacques takes advantage of John's commitment. First, he sits forward slightly. As John leans further forward for his pass, Jean Jacques changes his grip. With his left hand on John's collar and his right hand now grabbing the back of the gi, he shifts his body to his right and pulls John forward as if to help him pass.

3 He then grabs John's right hand with his left hand again and breaks John's grip on his left pants by keeping a stiff left arm. At the same time, he circles his left leg to the right until it reaches the other side of John's hips. Notice that without support, John starts falling to his right.

4 Jean Jacques plants his left hand on the mat and increases John's forward momentum to the right, pulling him by the back and forcing him face down on the mat. John ends up on all fours to brace. Otherwise, he would have his face on the mat.

5 Jean Jacques takes John's back as he gets to his knees while using his right arm to hold around John's waist and his left hand to hold John's left elbow.

64

Reversal from the butterfly guard 7: taking the back to the choke

Jean Jacques demonstrates a great attack from the butterfly guard. In this case, Jean Jacques goes from a guard defense to taking the back, not only scoring 6 points (2 for the reversal and 4 for taking the back because he puts the hooks in this time) but also achieving prime position for a fight-ending choke. The key to this move is to bait the opponent into putting his weight forward to overcome your knee block on the hips and to release the pressure of the block quickly, causing him to fall forward.

1 John is attempting to pass Jean Jacques's butterfly guard. He is holding John's gi sleeves with his hands.

2 Jean Jacques slides his hips to his right, releases the right foot hook, and changes his left hand grip from John's right sleeve to his left one.

3 Jean Jacques drops his back to the mat, pulling John's left arm with him, and places his right shin to block John's hips.

172

FIGHTING TECHNIQUES FIGHTING TECHNIQUES FIGHTING TECHNIQUES FIGHTING TECHNI
ING TECHNIQUES FIGHTING TECHNIQUES FIGHTING TECHNIQUES FIGHTIN
ES FIGHTING TECHNIQUES FIGHTING TECHNIQUES FIGHTING TECHNIQUES
TECHNIQUES FIGHTING TECHNIQUES FIGHTING TECHNIQUES FIGHTING TE
GHTING TECHNIQUES FIGHTING TECHNIQUES FIGHTING TECHNIQUES FIGH
IQUES FIGHTING TECHNIQUES FIGHTING TECHNIQUES FIGHTING TECHNIQ

4 In his attempt to pass the guard and get to Jean Jacques's right side, John drives his weight forward and uses his right hand to push Jean Jacques's knee down to remove the obstacle. If Jean Jacques weren't to react, John would simply push the leg down, extend his body so his hips would pin Jean Jacques's legs flat on the mat, and scoot around to his side for the guard pass. Jean Jacques pulls John's left arm across his body and places his left foot in front of John's left knee.

5 Jean Jacques pushes John's left knee with his left leg, removes his right shin from in front of John's hips, and pulls John's left arm up toward his head. John falls flat on the mat. Notice that Jean Jacques already has his left hook in place for taking the back. The key here is to keep the opponent's arm extended so he doesn't regroup and come back to all fours. If he does that, you will only score the reversal as you will not be able to place the other hook for the back control.

6 Jean Jacques loops his right leg over John's body and hooks his right foot in front of John's right hip. At the same time, he loops his right arm around John's neck, grabbing the left gi collar, and his left arm hooks inside John's left arm until the back of his hand touches the back of John's head. Jean Jacques applies the choke by opening his right elbow, pulling John's collar, and sliding his forearm behind John's head.

65
Half-guard attack to key lock

In keeping with Jean Jacques's philosophy of attacking whenever possible, here we demonstrate a key lock from the half-guard. This technique is a good complement to the previous one, should the defender manage to get ahead of you and get tight before you are able to pull his arm across, or in case he is passing with the arm hooked under your armpit.

1 John is inside Jean Jacques's half-guard and has his left arm hooked under Jean Jacques's right arm in his attempt to pass the guard. Jean Jacques has his left leg inside John's legs and his right shin in front of John's hips to block his hips and his forward progress and pass the guard.

2 Jean Jacques wraps his right arm around John's left arm. His left hand delivers John's right collar to his right hand.

3 Jean Jacques pushes John away by driving his right knee forward, creating some distance. Jean Jacques blocks John's right arm from grabbing his own collar with his left hand. Should John be able to grab Jean Jacques's collar, Jean Jacques would be unable to execute the submission and John would gain significant control.

4 Detail Notice Jean Jacques's right hand gripping John's right collar and his forearm wrapped around John's arm near the elbow. Should Jean Jacques have wrapped around John's forearm, he would not have had the proper leverage to force the elbow in and the wrist out.

4 Jean Jacques applies the key lock by arching his torso back toward his right, driving John's wrist toward the mat and the elbow up, applying pressure to John's left shoulder.

66
Closed guard attack 1: armlock variations

In this technique, Jean Jacques attempts an armlock but Todd quickly defends by pulling his arm back until his elbow passes Jean Jacques's hips. Jean Jacques cleverly switches to his second armlock attack.

1 Jean Jacques has Todd in his closed guard. He begins his attack by holding Todd's gi sleeves just above the elbows.

2 While still holding Todd's sleeves, Jean Jacques opens his legs, plants his left foot on the mat, and pushes off it to slide his hips to his left. At the same time, he lifts his right leg until his thigh locks under Todd's left armpit.

3 Jean Jacques passes his left leg in front of Todd's face, presses down on his calves, driving Todd's torso down, and lifts his hips up for the armlock.

4 The wily Todd quickly pulls his right arm out until his elbow passes Jean Jacques's hips, successfully defending the armlock.

NIQUES FIGHTING TECHNIQUES FIGHTING TECHNIQUES FIGHTING T
ING TECHNIQUES FIGHTING TECHNIQUES FIGHTING TECHNIQUES FIG
ES FIGHTING TECHNIQUES FIGHTING TECHNIQUES FIGHTING TECHNI
TECHNIQUES FIGHTING TECHNIQUES FIGHTING TECHNIQUES FIGHTING TI
GHTING TECHNIQUES FIGHTING TECHNIQUES FIGHTING TECHNIQUES FIGH
IQUES FIGHTING TECHNIQUES FIGHTING TECHNIQUES FIGHTING TECHNIC

5 Jean Jacques plants his right foot on Todd's left hip, escapes his hips back to center, and turns his left leg so that his shin touches Todd's face. Todd releases his right arm, assuming he is out of danger. Jean Jacques still controls Todd's left gi sleeve.

6 Pushing off his right leg, Jean Jacques continues moving his hips out to his right and lifts them so they lock just under Todd's left armpit. Notice that Jean Jacques's hip escape to his right positions his hips perfectly under Todd's arm.

7 Jean Jacques releases the right foot from Todd's hips and circles the right leg in front of Todd's face. Notice his left shin is locked under Todd's chin with his left foot hooked behind Todd's head, preventing Todd from pulling his torso and arm back.

8 Jean Jacques locks his right leg over and in front of Todd's face and presses it down as he lifts the hips, applying pressure on Todd's left elbow for the armlock.

TECHNIQUES FIGHTING TECHNIQUES FIGHTING TECHNIQUES FIGHTING TECHN
FIGHTING TECHNIQUES FIGHTING TECHNIQUES FIGHTING TECHNIQUES FIGHTI
TECHNIQUES FIGHTING TECHNIQUES FIGHTING TECHNIQUES FIGHTING TECHNIQUE
FIGHTING TECHNIQUES FIGHTING TECHNIQUES FIGHTING TECHNIQUES FIGHTING TE
IQUES FIGHTING TECHNIQUES FIGHTING TECHNIQUES FIGHTING TECHNIQUES FIG
NG TECHNIQUE FIGHTING TECHNIQUES FIGHTING TECHNIQUES FIGHTING TECHNIC

67

Closed guard attack 2: armlock and sweep combination

Jean Jacques demonstrates another armlock from the guard that is particularly effective when your opponent has his arm around your neck. Because this situation arises often, you should be alert to the opening and try the move right away. It will yield reversals, points for taking the back, and submissions.

1 Jean Jacques has John in his closed guard. John has his right arm around Jean Jacques's neck, a situation that may have occurred because Jean Jacques pulled John forward with his legs and arms, breaking his posture as he attempted to pass the guard. Jean Jacques's arms are wrapped around John's back.

2 Jean Jacques circles his left arm around John's right arm, bringing his left hand close to his own neck to lock the arm.

3 Jean Jacques opens his legs, plants his left foot on the ground and pushes off it to slide his hips to the left. Notice that Jean Jacques has John's right arm trapped by his left arm and head.

4 Jean Jacques bends his left leg and inserts his left foot on John's right hip and continues to slide his body to his left. Jean Jacques turns his head to his left, trapping John's right arm even tighter.

5 Jean Jacques pushes off his left leg, turns on his side, and arches his torso back, extending John's arm. Jean Jacques's left arm is already on top of John's arm. He now places it on John's elbow, locking his right arm over the left and pulling down and applying pressure on John's elbow.

5 Detail Notice how Jean Jacques locks his arms around John's arm on the elbow and how Jean Jacques's head is tilted up, keeping John from pulling his wrist out. The pressure on John's elbow will make him submit. At this point, an opponent sometimes manages to release his wrist and circle his right arm around your head. You would then take his back. A second defense is to push forward and hug the attacker, as John will demonstrate in the following technique.

179

68

Closed guard attack 2: armlock and sweep (continuation)

This continuation of the previous technique shows Jean Jacques's response to John's hug defense of the armlock.

1 John defends by pushing his weight forward and attempts to hug Jean Jacques.

2 Jean Jacques releases his armlock around John's elbow and reaches with his right hand to grab John's left triceps. Notice that Jean Jacques still has his left foot hooked on John's right hip, and his right leg is open near John's left leg.

FIGHTING TECHNIQUES FIGHTING TECHNIQUES FIGHTING TECHNIQUES FIGHTING TECHNI
NIQUES FIGHTING TECHNIQUES FIGHTING TECHNIQUES FIGHTING TECHNI
TING TECHNIQUES FIGHTING TECHNIQUES FIGHTING TECHNIQUES FIGHTIN
ES FIGHTING TECHNIQUES FIGHTING TECHNIQUES FIGHTING TECHNIQUES
TECHNIQUES FIGHTING TECHNIQUES FIGHTING TECHNIQUES FIGHTING TI
GHTIN   QUES FIGHTING TECHNIQUES FIGH
IQUES   G TECHNIQUES FIGHTING TECHNIC

3 Jean Jacques scissors his legs: he kicks his right leg in and kicks his left leg over, sweeping John to his right. Since John's left arm is blocked by Jean Jacques's right hand, and his left knee has been blocked by Jean Jacques's right leg kicking in, John falls to the mat.

4 Jean Jacques follows John over, still keeping the left foot hooked on John's hip and the lock on both arms . . .

5 Until he lands on top with a reversal.

TING TECHNIQUES FIGHTING TECHNIQUES FIGHTING TECHNIQUES FIGHTIN
JES FIGHTING TECHNIQUES FIGHTING TECHNIQUES FIGHTING TECHNIQUE
TECHNIQUES FIGHTING TECHNIQUES FIGHTING TECHNIQUES FIGHTING TE
FIGHTING TECHNIQUES FIGHTING TECHNIQUES FIGHTING TECHNIQUES FIG
NIQUES FIGHTING TECHNIQUES FIGHTING TECHNIQUES FIGHTING TECHNI
NG TECHNIQUES FIGHTING TECHNIQUES FIGHTING TECHNIQUES FIGHTING

69

Closed guard attack 3: key lock

The key lock is one of the seldom-used but highly effective attacks from the guard. Opponents worry so much about armlocks and reversals that they will often allow a lock over their shoulder because they fail to anticipate it. Consequently, Jean Jacques likes this move because it not only surprises the opponent but also quickly ends the match.

1 Jean Jacques has John in his closed guard. His left hand is inside John's left collar and his right hand grabs John's left elbow.

2 Jean Jacques wants to end this match quickly, so he opens the guard.

3 He plants his right foot on the mat, opens his left leg out, and pushes his hips to his right as he pushes John's left elbow in with his right hand. With his left hand, Jean Jacques pushes John's collar against his throat, forcing him to go to his own right. Notice that as Jean Jacques slides his hips to his right, John ends up falling forward with Jean Jacques on his side.

4 Jean Jacques locks his legs again, looping his right leg over John's left shoulder, trapping it and closing the guard. Jean Jacques continues pushing John's collar against his throat with his left hand to keep John from trying to come back to center.

FIGHTING TECHNIQUES FIGHTING TECHNIQUES FIGHTING TECHNIQUES FIG
NIQUES FIGHTING TECHNIQUES FIGHTING TECHNIQUES FIGHTING TECHN
ING TECHNIQUES FIGHTING TECHNIQUES FIGHTING TECHNIQUES FIGHTIN
ES FIGHTING TECHNIQUES FIGHTING TECHNIQUES FIGHTING TECHNIQUES
TECHNIQUES FIGHTING TECHNIQUES FIGHTING TECHNIQUES FIGHTING TI
GHTING TECHNIQUES FIGHTING TECHNIQUES FIGHTING TECHNIQUES FIG
IQUES FIGHTING TECHNIQUES FIGHTING TECHNIQUES FIGHTING TECHNIQ

5 Jean Jacques replaces his left hand with his right and continues to drive the collar against John's throat. His left arm circles around John's left forearm. Notice that John's elbow is on the mat and he cannot bring it back because it is being blocked by Jean Jacques's hips.

6 Jean Jacques opens his legs, looping his right leg over John's head.

7 Jean Jacques kicks his left leg up, driving John's right arm with it, and locks his right foot under the arm. Throughout the sequence, Jean Jacques pushes John's collar against his throat to keep him away.

8 Once he has locked his foot on John's right arm, Jean Jacques lets go of the collar and pulls John's left forearm up with both hands, forcing the shoulder lock. Notice that John's arm pivots around the elbow like a key lock. Jean Jacques pulls it up and to his own left for the pressure.

FIGHTING TECHNIQUES FIGHTING TECHNIQUES FIGHTING TECHNIQUES FIGHTING TECHN TING TECHNIQUES FIGHTING TECHNIQUES FIGHTING TECHNIQUES FIGHTING TECHNIQUES FIGHTI UES FIGHTING TECHNIQUES FIGHTING TECHNIQUES FIGHTING TECHNIQUES FIGHTING TECHNIQUE TECHNIQUE FIGHTING TECHNIQUES FIGHTING TECHNIQUES FIGHTING TECHNIQUES FIGHTING TE FIGHTING TECHNIQUES FIGHTING TECHNIQUES FIGHTING TECHNIQUES FIGHTING TECHNIQUES FIG NIQUES FIGHTING TECHNIQUES FIGHTING TECHNIQUES FIGHTING TECHNIQUES FIGHTING TECHNIC ING TECHNIQUES FIGHTING TECHNIQUES FIGHTING TECHNIQUES FIGHTING TECHNIQUES FIGHTING

70
Closed guard attack 4: omoplata

The omoplata is a very effective attack from the closed guard. In this case, John may be ahead in the fight and is stalling to use up time. He is inside Jean Jacques's closed guard and has good posture with his arms on Jean Jacques's chest to prevent him from sitting up to initiate any attacks, such as a choke or a cross-arm sweep. Or John may be setting up to pass Jean Jacques's guard. Regardless, Jean Jacques wants to press the action and decides to go for the shoulder lock.

1 John is inside Jean Jacques's guard and in good posture with his arms on Jean Jacques's chest. Jean Jacques crosses his left hand over and grabs John's left sleeve while he circles his right hand under John's left wrist.

2 Jean Jacques breaks John's posture by driving his right arm up and using his left hand to pull John's arm toward his head.

3 Jean Jacques continues to circle his right arm under John's left arm as he pulls it up and over his head with the left hand. Jean Jacques begins to open his guard as he unlocks his feet. Notice that Jean Jacques slid his head and right arm inside the circle made by his own left arm and John's left arm.

4 Pushing off his left calf on John's right hip, Jean Jacques kicks his right leg up, driving John farther forward until he is able to reach around with his right arm.

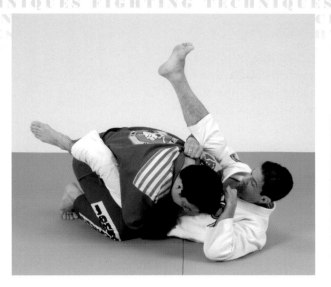

5 Jean Jacques grabs John's gi collar at the back of the neck with his right hand. At this point, Jean Jacques has John's left arm trapped between his right leg and arm and is in full control of John's torso. John cannot release his arm or lift his body.

6 Jean Jacques escapes his hips to his right as he braces his left hand on John's right biceps and drives his left knee in front of John's chest and right arm. Notice that Jean Jacques is lying on his left side.

7 Jean Jacques brings his right leg around and over John's head. He may use his left arm to help pull the leg around until the shin is in front of John's left ear.

8 Still grabbing the back of John's collar, Jean Jacques continues to circle his body around John's left shoulder, sits up by using his left arm on the mat, and brings his left leg out flat, achieving the shoulder lock position. From here, Jean Jacques lifts his hips, applying a great deal of pressure to John's left shoulder for the submission.

TING TECHNIQUES FIGHTING TECHNIQUES FIGHTING TECHNIQUES FIGHTI
UES FIGHTING TECHNIQUES FIGHTING TECHNIQUES FIGHTING TECHNIQUE
TECHNIQUES FIGHTING TECHNIQUES FIGHTING TECHNIQUES FIGHTING TE
FIGHTING TECHNIQUES FIGHTING TECHNIQUES FIGHTING TECHNIQUES FIG
NIQUES FIGHTING TECHNIQUES FIGHTING TECHNIQUES FIGHTING TECHNI
ING TECHNIQUES FIGHTING TECHNIQUES FIGHTING TECHNIQUES FIGHTING

71

Closed guard attack 5: biceps cutter

Jean Jacques loves to submit and his opponents know it. As a result, they often take defensive postures that require Jean Jacques to create novel ways to apply known submissions. In this case, Jean Jacques attempts three submission attempts in a row until John falls for one. First, he goes from the closed guard to what would initially appear to be a regular armlock from the guard as he dominates John's right arm. John defends by locking his hands together. Jean Jacques then tries for an omoplata. Again John defends, keeping his right arm closed. So Jean Jacques opts for the biceps cutter.

1 Jean Jacques has John in his closed guard and begins to attack the right arm. He wraps it with his left arm and readies himself for the armlock. John senses the danger and defends by locking his hands together and leaning forward to keep his forearm close to his chest.

2 Jean Jacques opens the guard and plants his right foot on the mat, using it to push his torso to the left.

186

NIQUES FIGHTING TECHNIQUES FIGHTING TECHNIQUES FIGHTING TECHNI
ING TECHNIQUES FIGHTING TECHNIQUES FIGHTING TECHNIQUES FIGHTIN
ES FIGHTING TECHNIQUES FIGHTING TECHNIQUES FIGHTING TECHNIQUES
TECHNIQUES FIGHTING TECHNIQUES FIGHTING TECHNIQUES FIGHTING TI
GHTIN   QUES FIGHTING TECHNIQUES FIGH
IQUES   G TECHNIQUES FIGHTING TECHNIQ

3 Jean Jacques starts to loop his left leg around John's right arm. John senses an attack to his right shoulder (the omoplata) and pulls his right arm close while blocking Jean Jacques's right leg with his left forearm.

4 Jean Jacques locks his right leg around John's right arm and uses both his hands to grab, preventing John from pulling the arm out. At this point, John is anticipating the omoplata and doesn't see the real threat.

5 Jean Jacques locks his right leg over the left foot for a figure-four around John's right arm. John's omoplata worries vanish, replaced by the pressure of the biceps cutter as Jean Jacques closes his legs and pulls his left forearm against John's biceps for the submission.

72

Closed guard attack 5 (continuation): opponent defends biceps cutter

In this continuation of the previous technique, John properly reacts to the biceps cutter by lifting Jean Jacques's hips off the mat. This defense decreases the pressure that Jean Jacques can apply as John stacks Jean Jacques. Jean Jacques uses John's reaction against him to reverse and submit him.

1 Jean Jacques has locked his legs in a figure-four around John's right arm and is ready to apply the pressure on the right arm for the biceps cutter.

2 John immediately reacts and defends the cruncher by leaning back, lifting Jean Jacques's hips off the mat, and stacking him. Now Jean Jacques cannot straighten his legs to apply the pressure for the cutter.

3 Jean Jacques takes advantage of John's reaction, using John's momentum and weight, which is all on his right side. Jean Jacques plants his right hand on the mat and kicks his legs over his head as he rolls over his left shoulder.

4 Jean Jacques continues to roll, taking John down to the mat with him. Once John begins to fall back to the mat, Jean Jacques open his right leg, releasing the figure-four . . .

5 And lands mounted on John. Notice that Jean Jacques lands with his right leg over John's head. It doesn't matter whether the leg is over or under John's left arm. Jean Jacques plants his left elbow on the mat, props himself up, and moves his hips to his left until his hips are under John's right arm. Notice that Jean Jacques retains control over John's right arm with his own right arm, grabbing behind the elbow to prevent John from yanking the elbow out.

6 Jean Jacques locks his left leg over John's head, lifts his hips, and pulls John's right arm for the armlock.

FIGHTING TECHNIQUES FIGHTING TECHNIQUES

73

Open guard attack: reverse triangle

The reverse triangle is a seldom used, yet very effective attack from the open guard. Jean Jacques likes it especially because of its rarity. It will not only surprise your opponent, but also open up a variety of submissions—so many, in fact, that we will divide this technique into two parts.

1 Jean Jacques has John in his open guard. His right foot presses against John's left biceps while his left shin blocks John's hips. Jean Jacques holds John's sleeves with his hands.

2 Jean Jacques quickly releases his right foot from John's left arm and throws it to his left as he turns his body in the same direction.

3 Jean Jacques brings the right leg down on top of John's neck, forcing John down. Jean Jacques spins his body to his left and releases his left shin from John's hip. Notice that Jean Jacques pulls John's left arm to help lock the position. Notice also the two keys to locking the figure-four: 1) Jean Jacques twists his hips clockwise as he releases the left shin, and 2) he brings his upper body to his left by bringing his head toward his left—as if he wanted to touch John's right knee. It would be very difficult to lock the reverse triangle if he stayed square in front of John.

4 Jean Jacques uses his right leg to lock the figure-four around John's left arm and head by locking his right foot under his left knee. He then pulls John's left arm across to help adjust the lock.

5 After he has locked John in the reverse triangle, Jean Jacques uses both arms to bring John's right arm around.

6 He wraps his right arm under the elbow and locks John's wrist between his neck and left shoulder. He applies the armlock by pulling down on the elbow with both arms as he lifts his torso.

74

Open guard attack (continuation): reverse triangle submission options

In this continuation from the previous technique, John has defended the arm by locking his hands around Jean Jacques's right leg, or they ended up this way in the scramble and Jean Jacques locked the reverse triangle. Jean Jacques has a reversal and two submissions from which to choose.

1 Should John somehow remove his arm and clasp both hands around Jean Jacques's right leg, Jean Jacques would place his left hand on John's left knee, keeping him from opening up, and push John's right hip with his right hand, forcing John to fall to his left.

2 Jean Jacques ends up mounted on John with his right knee up. Notice Jean Jacques's left-hand position on John's right knee. This was the block that prevented John from opening the leg out to brace and avoid the reversal.

FIGHTING TECHNIQUES FIGHTING TECHNIQUES FIGHTING TECHNIQUES FIGHTING TECHNI
NIQUES FIGHTING TECHNIQUES FIGHTING TECHNIQUES FIGHTING TECHNIQUES FIGHTING TECHNI
ING TECHNIQUES FIGHTING TECHNIQUES FIGHTING TECHNIQUES FIGHTING TECHNIQUES FIGHTIN
ES FIGHTING TECHNIQUES FIGHTING TECHNIQUES FIGHTING TECHNIQUES FIGHTING TECHNIQUES
TECHNIQUES FIGHTING TECHNIQUES FIGHTING TECHNIQUES FIGHTING TECHNIQUES FIGHTING T
GHTIN
QUES FIGHTING TECHNIQUES FIGH
IQUES
G TECHNIQUES FIGHTING TECHNI

3 Jean Jacques grabs John's right wrist with his left hand and wraps his right arm around John's right arm. He then locks his right hand on his own left wrist for the Kimura lock. He could apply pressure to the shoulder by driving John's wrist in a clockwise motion as if he wanted to touch John's right ear with the hand.

4 Alternately, Jean Jacques may at this point decide to go for the armlock instead of the Kimura. With the same lock around John's right arm, Jean Jacques kneels down with his right knee as he turns his body to his left. He plants his right foot on the mat and lifts the right knee as he starts to sit back toward the mat.

5 Jean Jacques finishes with the perfect armlock as he pulls John's right arm toward the mat and raises his hips, applying pressure on the elbow.

TECHNIQUES FIGHTING TECHNIQUES FIGHTING TECHNIQUES FIGHTING TECHNI FIGHTING TECHNIQUES FIGHTING TECHNIQUES FIGHTING TECHNIQUES FIGHTI ING TECHNIQUES FIGHTING TECHNIQUES FIGHTING TECHNIQUES FIGHTING TECHNIQUE FIGHTING TECHNIQUES FIGHTING TECHNIQUES FIGHTING TECHNIQUE TECHNIQUES FIGHTING TECHNIQUES FIGHTING TECHNIQUES FIGHTING TE TECHNIQUES FIGHTING TECHNIQUES FIGHTING TECHNIQUES FIGHTING TECHNIQUES FIGHTING TECHNIQUES FIGHTING TECHNIQUES FIC TECHNIQUES FIGHTING TECHNIQUES FIGHTING TECHNIQUES FIGHTING TECHNIC FIGHTING TECHNIQUES FIGHTING TECHNIQUES FIGHTING TECHNI TECHNIQUES FIGHTING

75

Side-control attack: S-mount to armlock

Frequently in matches, you obtain side control but your opponent turns to one side away from you. This may be the precursor for him to turn to all fours and escape the position, but it also offers a few options for attacks. Here, John cleverly goes for the S-mount and follows it with a quick submission.

1 John is across-side on Dion. Dion has turned to his right and brought his left knee and elbow close. John is holding Dion's left biceps and pushing his left elbow on Dion's thigh to prevent him from turning over to all fours.

2 John grips Dion's left gi pants at the knee, puts his right hand on the shoulder, and pushes off his arms to place his left knee on Dion's side, as in a knee-on-stomach. Because Dion is on his side, no points are awarded but rather an advantage is counted.

3 Still pushing down on his arms, John sits with his left buttock on Dion's left ribcage. At this point, John's weight should be on Dion's ribs.

4 John leans to his left and circles his left leg over Dion's head. Notice how he pivots on his buttocks and left hand. It is very important for John to use his weight on these pivot points, not only to help him execute the move, but also to keep Dion from moving.

5 John finishes the S-mount with his left leg in front of Dion's stomach. John has the outside blade of his left foot touching the mat. Still with his weight on his pivot points (left arm and buttocks), John circles his right arm around Dion's left arm. Notice John's left hand pushing down on Dion's left knee, pinning his legs to the mat.

6 Once he controls Dion's left arm, John starts to spin his body to his right. John still holds on to Dion's left pants, preventing him from escaping to his right, and begins to fall to the mat.

7 As his back starts to hit the mat, John circles his right leg until it is over Dion's face and prepares to lock over it for the armlock. John releases his left hand from Dion's gi pants and grabs around the thigh.

8 John passes his right leg in front of Dion's face and extends his torso while lifting his hips and applying pressure to Dion's left elbow for the armlock. By holding Dion's left leg, John prevents him from sliding his hips and rolling over the top for a defense.

195

76

Across-side attack: collar choke

Being across-side on an opponent is a very good and stable position. Not only is it much harder to reverse someone from there than from the mount, but the side control position also offers a large number of attacks and submissions. John demonstrates here a couple of sneaky chokes that use the gi collar.

1 John is across-side on Jean Jacques. His right arm is wrapped under Jean Jacques's head, and his shoulder pushes against Jean Jacques's chin, preventing him from turning into John to initiate an escape. John's left arm is under Jean Jacques's right arm with his hand holding the shoulder for control. John's chest presses against Jean Jacques to flatten him on the mat, further hindering Jean Jacques from beginning any escape action, such as a hip escape. If possible, John already has his own right gi lapel open.

2 As discretely as possible, John grabs and pulls his right gi lapel as close to the end as he can. It is important for John to grab close to the end so that he can complete the next move without hitting Jean Jacques's head.

3 John circles his right arm around Jean Jacques's head, sliding his right hand on the mat until he has the edge of the collar on Jean Jacques's right side. Notice that John opens his elbow out to facilitate bringing the collar under Jean Jacques's head.

4 John closes his right elbow in and drops and drives his forearm down on Jean Jacques's throat for the choke. The choking action is performed by the combination of John's collar around the neck and his right forearm across Jean Jacques's throat.

5 As a variation, John opts to slide his right arm under Jean Jacques's head. This option works well if your gi is tight or if you would have difficulty getting the loop around the opponent's head because the opponent is big or your arm is relatively short.

6 John feeds the collar to his left hand . . .

7 And pulls his right arm from under Jean Jacques's head while maintaining pressure with his torso on Jean Jacques's chest to keep him from turning and escaping.

8 John then takes the collar back with his right hand and drives his forearm down on Jean Jacques's throat for the choke. In both cases, you can increase the pressure of the choke by pushing your torso forward, tightening the collar around the neck.

FIGHTING TECHNIQUES FIGHTING TECHNIQUES FIGHTING TECHNIQUES FIGHTI
TING TECHNIQUES FIGHTING TECHNIQUES FIGHTING TECHNIQUES FIGHTI
UES FIGHTING TECHNIQUES FIGHTING TECHNIQUES FIGHTING TECHNIQUE
TECHNIQUES FIGHTING TECHNIQUES FIGHTING TECHNIQUES FIGHTING TE
FIGHTING TECHNIQUES FIGHTING TECHNIQUES FIGHTING TECHNIQUES FIC
NIQUES FIGHTING TECHNIQUES FIGHTING TECHNIQUES FIGHTING TECHNIC
ING TECHNIQUES FIGHTING TECHNIQUES FIGHTING TECHNIQUES FIGHTING

77

Attacking the turtle: choke (opponent facing)

Turning turtle (going to the all-fours position) is a common situation in a
match. In one instance, an opponent might turn to all fours to keep from
having points scored from a guard pass. In another, the opponent might
turn turtle as an escape from side control. John demonstrates a very solid
submission from that position, one that is especially effective when applied
just as the opponent starts to reach the turtle position.

1 Dion has turned turtle in front
of John. John has sprawled and
uses his chest to press Dion's back.

2 John wraps his left arm
under Dion's right arm, close
to the armpit, until he passes his
hand in front of Dion's neck. John
continues to press the weight of
his body against Dion's back to
keep him pinned.

FIGHTING TECHNIQUES FIGHTING TECHNIQUES FIGHTING TECHNIQUES FIGHTING TECHNIQUES FIGHTING TECHN
NIQUES FIGHTING TECHNIQUES FIGHTING TECHNIQUES FIGHTING TECHNIQUES FIGHTING TECHN
ING TECHNIQUES FIGHTING TECHNIQUES FIGHTING TECHNIQUES FIGHTING TECHNIQUES FIGHTIN
ES FIGHTING TECHNIQUES FIGHTING TECHNIQUES FIGHTING TECHNIQUES FIGHTING TECHNIQUES
TECHNIQUES FIGHTING TECHNIQUES FIGHTING TECHNIQUES FIGHTING TECHNIQUES FIGHTING TE
GHTIN FIGHTING TECHNIQUES FIGH
NIQUES NIQUES FIGHTING TECHNIC

3 John slides his right arm toward Dion's head, clasps his hands together, palms facing each other, and brings his elbows together.

4 John steps in with his right foot in front of Dion's head, plants his left foot over Dion's right leg, and sits back, pulling Dion with him.

5 As he continues to sit back on the mat, John tightens the choke by bringing his elbows together and pushing his face onto Dion's left shoulder. Notice how John trapped Dion's right leg with his left foot to prevent him from walking around to his left and releasing the choking pressure.

TING TECHNIQUES FIGHTING TECHNIQUES FIGHTING TECHNIQUES FIGHTI
UES FIGHTING TECHNIQUES FIGHTING TECHNIQUES FIGHTING TECHNIQUE
TECHNIQUES FIGHTING TECHNIQUES FIGHTING TECHNIQUES FIGHTING TE
FIGHTING TECHNIQUES FIGHTING TECHNIQUES FIGHTING TECHNIQUES FIG
NIQUES FIGHTING TECHNIQUES FIGHTING TECHNIQUES FIGHTING TECHNIC
ING TECHNIQUES FIGHTING TECHNIQUES FIGHTING TECHNIQUES FIGHTING

78

Mounted position attack: armlock

The mounted position is one of the most dominant positions in Brazilian jiu-jitsu. Once you've attained it, the first and most important thing is to maintain it. The next is to capitalize on it for a submission. Here, Jean Jacques is mounted on John and goes for a variation of the armlock. He starts the move with a key-lock feign to John's right arm. Once John focuses on defending the right, Jean Jacques will actually attack the left arm. Once again, it is important to execute the first attack with the full intention of success. If the opponent defends correctly, then and only then should you attempt your other option.

1 Jean Jacques is mounted on John. John has good defensive posture with his elbows close to his torso, keeping Jean Jacques from climbing up on his body, and his hands protecting the collar to defend the choke.

2 Jean Jacques uses his left arm to push down on John's right arm as if he wanted to apply a key lock. John reacts and turns his attention to that arm, pulling it tight against his chest. With his right hand, Jean Jacques now pulls up on John's left arm, separating it slightly from the chest. Jean Jacques cannot go directly to the standard armlock from the mount because John's arm is not stretched out enough. Should he attempt that, he may lose the top position and John's arm at the same time. Instead, Jean Jacques uses this variation of the armlock.

3 Jean Jacques puts his weight on his right knee, circles his leg over John's head (see drill 7, circling the legs) as he leans to his right, and continues to pull John's left arm.

FIGHTING TECHNIQUES FIGHTING TECHNIQUES FIGHTING TECHNIQUES FIGHTING TECHNI
NIQUES FIGHTING TECHNIQUES FIGHTING TECHNIQUES FIGHTING TECHNIQUES FIGHTING TECHNI
ING TECHNIQUES FIGHTING TECHNIQUES FIGHTING TECHNIQUES FIGHTING TECHNIQUES FIGHTIN
ES FIGHTING TECHNIQUES FIGHTING TECHNIQUES FIGHTING TECHNIQUES FIGHTING TECHNIQUES
TECHNIQUES FIGHTING TECHNIQUES FIGHTING TECHNIQUES FIGHTING TECHNIQUES FIGHTING T
GHTING TECHNIQUES FIGHTING TECHNIQUES FIGHTING TECHNIQUES FIGHTING TECHNIQUES FIGH
IQUES FIGHTING TECHNIQUES FIGHTING TECHNIQUES FIGHTING TECHNIQUES FIGHTING TECHNI

4 After his left foot passes over John's right arm and head, Jean Jacques plants it next to John's left ear, with his shin facing John's cheek.

5 Jean Jacques shifts his weight farther to his right, pulling John's left arm with him and hooking his left foot under John's head to prevent John from pushing the foot away with his right hand and escaping.

6 Jean Jacques then falls back, pulling John's arm with him and lifting John's head with his left foot hook.

7 Jean Jacques loops his right leg over John's face and pulls the right arm across his hips for the armlock.

TING TECHNIQUES FIGHTING TECHNIQUES FIGHTING TECHNIQUES FIGHTI
UES FIGHTING TECHNIQUES FIGHTING TECHNIQUES FIGHTING TECHNIQUE
TECHNIQ FIGHTING TECHNIQUES FIGHTING TECHNIQUES FIGHTING TE
FIGHTING TECHNIQUES FIGHTING TECHNIQUES FIGHTING TECHNIQUES FIC
NIQUES FIGHTING TECHNIQUES FIGHTING TECHNIQUES FIGHTING TECHNI
ING TECHNIQUES FIGHTING TECHNIQUES FIGHTING TECHNIQUES FIGHTING

79

Submission from the guard: choke

The two-hands-in-the-collar choke from the guard is perhaps the first submission everyone learns in BJJ. It is so common that the savvy competitor will usually be alert and defend it. As soon as the first hand goes in the collar, the defender can be counted on to block the other hand from coming in the opposite collar. Jean Jacques here shows us an alternative: a very clever and powerful choke from the guard. He begins by attempting a cross sweep, which Todd defends by lowering his head and hips to keep Jean Jacques down. As one of Jean Jacques's hands is gripping Todd's belt, Todd focuses on a possible sweep rather than anticipating a choke. Jean Jacques takes advantage of that.

1 Jean Jacques has Todd inside his guard, and Todd has his hands on Jean Jacques's chest. By moving his elbows up and down while keeping his hands on Jean Jacques's chest, Todd blocks every attempt Jean Jacques makes to put a hand in the collar.

2 Facing Todd's good defense, Jean Jacques opens his guard, places his right foot on the mat, moves his hips to his right, and reaches with his right arm in front of Todd's face to grab the belt. This movement is very similar to the cross sweep, where Jean Jacques would actually trap Todd's right arm with his own right arm and bump him over to the right with his hips.

3 Sensing the sweep attempt coming, Todd drives his torso down to keep Jean Jacques from coming up with his hips for the bump. This reaction helps Jean Jacques grab the belt. Should Todd have failed to react, Jean Jacques would have simply bumped him over for the sweep and the 2 points.

FIGHTING TECHNIQUES FIGHTING TECHNIQUES FIGHTING TECHNIQUES FI
NIQUES FIGHTING TECHNIQUES FIGHTING TECHNIQUES FIGHTING TECHNI
ING TECHNIQUES FIGHTING TECHNIQUES FIGHTING TECHNIQUES FIGHTIN
ES FIGHTING TECHNIQUES FIGHTING TECHNIQUES FIGHTING TECHNIQUES
TECHNIQUES FIGHTING TECHNIQUES FIGHTING TECHNIQUES FIGHTING TE
GHTING TECHNIQUES FIGHTING TECHNIQUES FIGHTING TECHNIQUES FIGH
IQUES FIGHTING TECHNIQUES FIGHTING TECHNIQUES FIGHTING TECHNIQ

4 Jean Jacques places both heels on the mat, slides his body back, and sits up to create some room between his hips and Todd.

5 He then slides his left hand inside Todd's left collar, with his palm facing up, his fingers inside the collar, and the thumb on the outside.

6 Jean Jacques closes his right elbow down, pressing against Todd's back and the back of his neck.

7 Jean Jacques turns his body to the right, pulls his left arm back, tightening the collar, and drives his right elbow down, applying great pressure for the choke.

80
Submission from the guard: armlock from an overhead sweep

Another great submission from an attempted sweep is shown here. As in technique 79, Jean Jacques tries for a sweep and then pursues another option, in this case the armlock, because of Todd's reaction and defense.

1 Jean Jacques has Todd in his closed guard. His right hand holds Todd's right collar and his left one is holding Todd's right sleeve. Again, Todd has his hands on Jean Jacques's chest for bracing and is able to use his elbows to block Jean Jacques's hands from coming inside the collar for a choke.

2 Jean Jacques initiates the action. He opens his legs, puts his right foot on the mat, and pushes off it, shifting his hips to the right.

3 Jean Jacques slides his right knee between his own right arm and Todd's left arm.

FIGHTING TECHNIQUES FIGHTING TECHNIQUES FIGHTING TECHNIQUES FIG
NIQUES FIGHTING TECHNIQUES FIGHTING TECHNIQUES FIGHTING TECHN
ING TECHNIQUES FIGHTING TECHNIQUES FIGHTING TECHNIQUES FIGHTIN
ES FIGHTING TECHNIQUES FIGHTING TECHNIQUES FIGHTING TECHNIQUES
TECHNIQUES FIGHTING TECHNIQUES FIGHTING TECHNIQUES FIGHTING T
GHTING TECHNIQUES FIGHTING TECHNIQUES FIGHTING TECHNIQUES FIG
IQUES FIGHTING TECHNIQUES FIGHTING TECHNIQUES FIGHTING TECHNIQ

4 He places his right foot on Todd's left hip and pushes off it to move his hips to the center as he lifts and coils his left leg.

5 Jean Jacques starts by placing his left foot on Todd's right hip and then the other foot on the opposite side. Once both feet are placed, Jean Jacques presses against the hips as if he wants to push Todd away. Todd's reaction is to press forward against the pressure. Notice that Jean Jacques still holds Todd's collar and right sleeve.

FIGHTING TECHNIQUES FIGHTING TECHNIQUES FIGHTING TECHNIQUES FIGHTING TECHN
TING TECHNIQUES FIGHTING TECHNIQUES FIGHTING TECHNIQUES FIGHTING TECHNIQUES FIGHTI
UES FIGHTING TECHNIQUES FIGHTING TECHNIQUES FIGHTING TECHNIQUE
TECHNIQUES FIGHTING TECHNIQUES FIGHTING TECHNIQUES FIGHTING TE
FIGHTING TECHNIQUES FIGHTING TECHNIQUES FIGHTING TECHNIQUES FIG
NIQUES FIGHTING TECHNIQUES FIGHTING TECHNIQUES FIGHTING TECHNI
ING TECHNIQUES FIGHTING TECHNIQUES FIGHTING TECHNIQUES FIGHTING

6 Using Todd's forward pressure against him, Jean Jacques quickly releases his own pressure on the hips and pulls up on Todd's collar and sleeve, bringing Todd toward Jean Jacques's head. Although Jean Jacques has released the full pressure on Todd's hips, he keeps his feet in place and uses them to help push the hips up for the overhead sweep. Todd reacts effectively: he extends his arms, pushes his body back down, and drives all his weight down toward the mat. Had Todd not defended the move, he would have been swept overhead.

7 Sensing the sweep defense, Jean Jacques quickly changes his approach. He releases his right foot from Todd's hips while pushing off his left one. He pivots his hips to his left and brings his right leg up under Todd's left arm.

NIQUES FIGHTING TECHNIQUES FIGHTING TECHNIQUES FIGHTING TECHNIQUES FIGHTING TECHNI
ING TECHNIQUES FIGHTING TECHNIQUES FIGHTING TECHNIQUES FIGHTING TECHNIQUES FIGHTIN
ES FIGHTING TECHNIQUES FIGHTING TECHNIQUES FIGHTING TECHNIQUES FIGHTING TECHNIQUES
TECHNIQUES FIGHTING TECHNIQUES FIGHTING TECHNIQUES FIGHTING TECHNIQUES FIGHTING TI
GHTING TECHNIQUES FIGHTING TECHNIQUES FIGHTING TECHNIQUES FIGHTING TECHNIQUES FIGH
IQUES FIGHTING TECHNIQUES FIGHTING TECHNIQUES FIGHTING TECHNIQUES FIGHTING TECHNIC

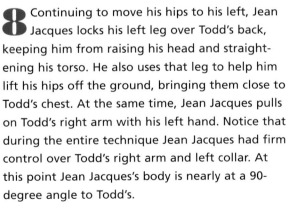

8 Continuing to move his hips to his left, Jean Jacques locks his left leg over Todd's back, keeping him from raising his head and straightening his torso. He also uses that leg to help him lift his hips off the ground, bringing them close to Todd's chest. At the same time, Jean Jacques pulls on Todd's right arm with his left hand. Notice that during the entire technique Jean Jacques had firm control over Todd's right arm and left collar. At this point Jean Jacques's body is nearly at a 90-degree angle to Todd's.

9 Jean Jacques passes his left leg in front of Todd's head and extends his body, driving his hip up against Todd's right elbow while pulling Todd's hand to his chest for the armlock. Notice that Jean Jacques does not extend his legs, but rather maintains the calves' pressure on Todd's back to keep him from standing up or yanking his arm out. Jean Jacques presses down on Todd with his calves, driving Todd's torso toward the mat as he drives his hips up and pulls the arm.

81

Submission from knee-on-stomach: choke

The knee-on-stomach is a great position from which to attack and submit your opponent. From there you can easily attack both arms and the neck for a choke. In this case, Jean Jacques goes for a normal choke, John blocks it, and Jean Jacques immediately changes strategy to use John's blocking arm for a novel variation of the choke with the same ultimate result.

1 Jean Jacques is in a classic knee-on-stomach position. His right leg is out, foot firmly planted on the mat, and his left knee presses down on John's stomach. His right hand pulls on John's left sleeve and his left hand is inside John's collar. From here, Jean Jacques can go for an armlock on John's right arm or release the grip and use his right hand to grab John's right collar for a choke.

2 Because John has his back flat on the mat, the arm attack is more difficult, so Jean Jacques decides to attack the neck. His right hand lets go of John's sleeve and reaches to grab John's right collar.

3 Seeing the attack, John quickly moves his right hand and parries Jean Jacques's wrist, blocking his path to the collar.

NIQUES FIGHTING TECHNIQUES FIGHTING TECHNIQUES FIGHTING TECHNI
ING TECHNIQUES FIGHTING TECHNIQUES FIGHTING TECHNIQUES FIGHTIN
ES FIGHTING TECHNIQUES FIGHTING TECHNIQUES FIGHTING TECHNIQUES
TECHNIQUES FIGHTING TECHNIQUES FIGHTING TECHNIQUES FIGHTING TI
GHTIN   UES FIGHTING TECHNIQUES FIGH
IQUE   TECHNIQUES FIGHTING TECHNIQ

4 Jean Jacques circles his hand around John's blocking hand . . .

5 And grabs the top of John's right sleeve, pulling it across John's body as he releases the pressure on the knee-on-stomach. Notice that because John is forced by Jean Jacques to turn to his own left, Jean Jacques's right hand is suddenly very deep in John's collar.

6 Jean Jacques drops his weight on his left shoulder, pushing down on John's right arm near the shoulder and driving it against John's neck. The combination of that pressure (shoulder on the arm and arm driven across the neck) and the tension Jean Jacques creates by pulling his own left hand up causes a tremendous choking pressure on John's neck.

TING TECHNIQUES FIGHTING TECHNIQUES FIGHTING TECHNIQUES FIGHTI
UES FIGHTING TECHNIQUES FIGHTING TECHNIQUES FIGHTING TECHNIQUE
TECHNI FIGHTING TECHNIQUES FIGHTING TECHNIQUES FIGHTING TE
FIGHTING TECHNIQUES FIGHTING TECHNIQUES FIGHTING TE
NIQUES GHTING TECHNIQUES FIGHTING TECHNI
ING TECHNIQUES FIGHTING TECHNIQUES

82

Submission from the all-fours position: cervical hold

In both sparring and competition, opponents often find themselves facing
each other on all fours. Here, Jean Jacques and John demonstrate two techniques at once, first the reversal as John reverses Jean Jacques by trapping his
arm, then the counter and submission as Jean Jacques applies the cervical
hold. Be extremely careful when applying the cervical hold, as damage to the
spine can occur. For that reason, the hold is illegal in some tournaments.

1 Both fighters are on all fours, but Jean Jacques controls the position from the top with his chest on John's back and his arms wrapped around John's chest. From here, Jean Jacques has a wide array of attack options he can run to either side and get to be on John's back and even without the hooks have a wide array of attacking possibilities.

2 John begins his escape by wrapping his right arm around Jean Jacques's left arm near the triceps. It is extremely important for John to wrap Jean Jacques's arm above the elbow; otherwise, Jean Jacques can pull the arm out easily.

3 John plants his left hand on the mat and pushes off it as he shoots his right knee in and rolls over his right shoulder, taking Jean Jacques with him.

FIGHTING TECHNIQUES FIGHTING TECHNIQUES FIGHTING TECHNIQUES FIGHTING TECHNI
TING TECHNIQUES FIGHTING TECHNIQUES FIGHTING TECHNIQUES FIGHTIN
ES FIGHTING TECHNIQUES FIGHTING TECHNIQUES FIGHTING TECHNIQUES
TECHNIQUES FIGHTING TECHNIQUES FIGHTING TECHNIQUES FIGHTING TI
GHTIN ES FIGHTING TECHNIQUES FIGH
IQUES TECHNIQUES FIGHTING TECHNI

4 Jean Jacques ends up on the bottom. His arms still grab John's chest to start the counter.

5 Jean Jacques uses his arms to pull John's arms open.

6 He loops his right leg over John's right arm. Notice that Jean Jacques pulls the arms at the elbows so John cannot simply spin the arms out.

211

TING TECHNIQUES FIGHTING TECHNIQUES FIGHTING TECHNIQUES FIGHTI
UES FIGHTING TECHNIQUES FIGHTING TECHNIQUES FIGHTING TECHNIQUE
TECHNIQUES FIGHTING TECHNIQUES FIGHTING TECHNIQUES FIGHTING TE
FIGHTING TECHNIQUES FIGHTING TECHNIQUES FIGHTING TECHNIQUES FIG
NIQUES F   TCHNIQUES FIGHTING TECHNI
NG TECH   TING TECHNIQUES FIGHTING

7 Jean Jacques locks a figure-four with his legs, left leg over the right foot, around John's right arm, trapping it completely. He turns his body to his left in a counterclockwise direction and wraps his right arm over John's left arm.

8 Jean Jacques continues to turn to his left as he rolls on to his stomach. Notice that the right side of Jean Jacques's ribcage is pushing against John's head.

9 Jean Jacques continues to turn in a counterclockwise direction and plants his elbows on the mat to raise his chest, using his ribcage to push John's head for the cervical hold.

FIGHTING TECHNIQUES FIGHTING TECHNIQUES FIGHTING TECHNIQUES FIGHTING TECHNI
NIQUES FIGHTING TECHNIQUES FIGHTING TECHNIQUES FIGHTING TECHNI
ING TECHNIQUES FIGHTING TECHNIQUES FIGHTING TECHNIQUES FIGHTIN
ES FIGHTING TECHNIQUES FIGHTING TECHNIQUES FIGHTING TECHNIQUES
TECHNIQUES FIGHTING TECHNIQUES FIGHTING TECHNIQUES FIGHTING TI
GHTIN FIGHTING TECHNIQUES FIGH
IQUES CHNIQUES FIGHTING TECHNIQ

10 As a variation, or in the event that cervical holds are illegal, Jean Jacques plants his left arm out and opens his legs, releasing the figure-four lock as he slides his left knee toward John's left shoulder. Notice that Jean Jacques still keeps his right leg over John's right arm for control.

11 Jean Jacques continues to push off his left arm until his left leg is past John's body. At this point, he has the left arm trapped and is ready to go for the armlock.

12 Jean Jacques loops his left leg over John's chest and pulls the left arm open across his hips for the armlock.

TING TECHNIQUES FIGHTING TECHNIQUES FIGHTING TECHNIQUES FIGHTI
UES FIGHTING TECHNIQUES FIGHTING TECHNIQUES FIGHTING TECHNIQUE
TECHNI FIGHTING TECHNIQUES FIGHTING TECHNIQUES FIGHTING TE
IGHTING TECHNIQUES FIGHTING TECHNIQUES FIGHTING TECHNIQUES FIG
NIQUES FIGHTING TECHNIQUES FIGHTING TECHNIQUES FIGHTING TECHNI
ING TECHNIQUES FIGHTING TECHNIQUES FIGHTING TECHNIQUES FIGHTING

83

Escaping from back control on all fours: side roll

While attacks are very important in training and competition, being able to escape from a difficult position may make the difference between winning and losing or between being submitted or not. Here, John uses the movement in drill 8, the side roll, to escape from back control on all fours. This is the perfect controlling position for Jean Jacques to attack John's neck with a clock choke.

1 John is on all fours with Jean Jacques on his back. From this position, Jean Jacques has many options. For example, he can take full back control with hooks and attain 4 points, or he can go for the "clock choke." None of the options are good for John. John's first concern is not to be submitted, so he uses both hands to block Jean Jacques's right hand from grabbing his collar. Notice Jean Jacques's controlling position: his left arm wrapped around John's back with the hand tucked on the hip or thigh. His right leg is open, increasing the pressure that his head and chest are exerting on John's back to keep him from standing up.

2 Once he has defended the neck attack, John opens his left arm and plants his left hand on the mat. His right hand, pushing down on Jean Jacques's right wrist, secures the wrist against the mat, deterring it from reaching the collar.

FIGHTING TECHNIQUES FIGHTING TECHNIQUES FIGHTING TECHNIQUES FIG
NIQUES FIGHTING TECHNIQUES FIGHTING TECHNIQUES FIGHTING TECHNI
ING TECHNIQUES FIGHTING TECHNIQUES FIGHTING TECHNIQUES FIGHTIN
ES FIGHTING TECHNIQUES FIGHTING TECHNIQUES FIGHTING TECHNIQUES
TECHNIQUES FIGHTING TECHNIQUES FIGHTING TECHNIQUES FIGHTING TI
GHTIN
HIQUES
ECHNIC
CING

3 John opens up his left leg and plants the left foot wide of his body.

4 John tucks his right arm between his legs as if he were reaching back, pushes off his left leg, and rolls over his right shoulder.

5 John continues to roll over his shoulder in a movement similar to drill 8, the side roll, forcing Jean Jacques forward with him. Jean Jacques must let go of his left-arm grip around John's waist or he will either be forced to roll over with John or end up in a shoulder lock much like the omoplata.

6 John continues to roll over his shoulder, separating himself from Jean Jacques, and plants his left foot and right hand on the mat to ready himself.

7 At the end of the roll, John has shed Jean Jacques from his back and is in base and ready to start to fight again. Jean Jacques ends up with his face on the mat or worse.

84

Escaping from back control on all fours: hip roll

In position 83, Jean Jacques was on John's back, applying his weight straight down to keep John from standing up to escape, and John escaped nonetheless by using the side roll. Here, as John starts to escape, Jean Jacques pushes him back to his left, keeping him from opening his left leg for the side roll. John will use Jean Jacques's move to his own advantage and go for the hip roll. This is another escape that can be used with the clock choke.

1 Jean Jacques is on John's back and attempting a clock choke. John uses his left hand to block Jean Jacques's right hand from grabbing his left collar for the choke. Jean Jacques could also be contemplating a crucifix as he uses his right hand to grip John's right wrist. (In the crucifix, he'd hook John's right arm with his right leg and John's left arm with his left arm and roll over to John's left, having John's arms trapped open like a crucifix.)

2 John tries to escape by leaning over to his right, but Jean Jacques pushes off his right leg and uses his chest to push John back. John circles his left arm around Jean Jacques's left arm and grabs the sleeve with his hand. Notice how John puts his right hand on his face to prevent Jean Jacques from hooking his right leg around the forearm and going for the crucifix.

3 Using Jean Jacques's momentum to the left, John shoots his right leg out between Jean Jacques's legs and pushes to the left (in a clockwise direction).

4 John continues to roll to his left as he tucks his left leg in, forcing Jean Jacques over the top with him. Jean Jacques's left arm is trapped and he cannot open it to brace and stop the movement.

5 John continues to roll to his left . . .

6 Until he lands on top of Jean Jacques in side control.

TECHNIQUES FIGHTING TECHNIQUES FIGHTING TECHNIQUES FIGHTING TECHNIQUES FIGHTI
TING TECHNIQUES FIGHTING TECHNIQUES FIGHTING TECHNIQUES FIGHTI
UES FIGHTING TECHNIQUES FIGHTING TECHNIQUES FIGHTING TECHNIQUE
TECHNIQUES FIGHTING TECHNIQUES FIGHTING TECHNIQUES FIGHTING TE
FIGHTING TECHNIQUES FIGHTING TECHNIQUES FIGHTING TECHNIQUES FIG
NIQUES FIGHTING TECHNIQUES FIGHTING TECHNIQUES FIGHTING TECHNI
ING TECHNIQUES FIGHTING TECHNIQUES FIGHTING TECHNIQUES FIGHTING

85
Escaping from back control on all fours: side roll (variation)

In this escape from the clock choke or back control, John reacts quickly
before Jean Jacques is able to plant his right leg out and put pressure on
the back. Since Jean Jacques has his knee on the ground, John is able to roll
him to his right and end up with a reversal. Notice that John only tries this
technique because Jean Jacques has his forward (right) knee on the ground
and does not have the ability to press against the back or react quickly by
stepping around with the right leg to block the roll.

1 John is on all fours with Jean Jacques on his
back. Jean Jacques has not opened his right leg
wide for base to apply pressure. John reacts quickly
and traps Jean Jacques's right arm, grabbing the
sleeve around the wrist and tucking it under.

2 John pushes Jean Jacques's arm between his legs
and begin to roll over his right shoulder.

3 Jean Jacques cannot brace with his right arm
and is forced to fall forward. Notice that by
driving Jean Jacques's right arm between his legs,
John brings Jean Jacques's right shoulder down,
upsetting his balance as well.

4 At this point, John needs additional force to prevent a stalemate in which Jean Jacques tries to
come back to the top. John opens his left leg and arm
out and pushes off them to force the roll over Jean
Jacques's body.

5 Pushing off his hand and foot, John kicks his leg over and jumps backwards over Jean Jacques.

6 John lands on the opposite side in side control. Notice that during this entire exchange John has retained hold of Jean Jacques's right arm, preventing him from bracing and pushing back. This will come in handy at this point because John has the perfect setup for a Kimura. His left hand grabs Jean Jacques's right wrist, pulling it up.

7 John wraps his right arm around Jean Jacques's right arm above the elbow and locks his right hand on his left wrist, setting up the submission.

8 John drives Jean Jacques's right arm to the mat, applying torque on the shoulder. Should Jean Jacques have good range of motion in his shoulder and not be forced to tap, John will turn his hips to face Jean Jacques's head and lift the elbow while keeping the wrist down. In the case of extreme flexibility of the shoulder joint, John would loop his right leg over Jean Jacques's head until his right foot touched beside Jean Jacques's right ear, and then lean back, lifting Jean Jacques's right shoulder and arm off the mat. Simultaneously, he would drive Jean Jacques's right wrist around in a clockwise direction.

FIGHTING TECHNIQUES FIGHTING TECHNIQUES

86

Escaping from top control on all fours 1: wrestler's escape

As it is so common for both fighters to end up on all fours facing each other, knowing how to escape this control is vital. Here, John demonstrates how to use the movement in drill 9, the wrestler's drill, to escape top control on all fours and how to continue toward your opponent's back.

1 Jean Jacques and John are both on all fours facing each other. Jean Jacques is on top with his chest pressing down on John's back, and his arms are wrapped around John's torso.

2 John steps out with his left leg and moves his head slightly to the same side.

220

FIGHTING TECHNIQUES FIGHTING TECHNIQUES FIGHTING TECHNIQUES FIGHTING TECHN
ING TECHNIQUES FIGHTING TECHNIQUES FIGHTING TECHNIQUES FIGHTIN
ES FIGHTING TECHNIQUES FIGHTING TECHNIQUES FIGHTING TECHNIQUES
TECHNIQUES FIGHTING TECHNIQUES FIGHTING TECHNIQUES FIGHTING TI
GHTING TECHNIQUES FIGHTING TECHNIQUES FIGHTING TECHNIQUES FIGH
NIQUES FIGHTING TECHNIQUES FIGHTING TECHNIQUES FIGHTING TECHNI

3 Bracing off his left foot and right elbow, John raises his left arm and shoots his right leg through the gap formed between the left foot and right arm. At the same time, John drives his head up under Jean Jacques's armpit. It is very important for John to keep his head close to Jean Jacques's torso as he goes for the next step.

4 John steps forward with his left leg as he reaches around toward Jean Jacques's back. Notice that John's right arm is already in perfect position to grab Jean Jacques's torso. His head pushes down on Jean Jacques's back, hindering him from getting up and helping John's movement toward Jean Jacques's back.

87

Escaping from top control on all fours 2 (opponent very strong)

A very strong opponent can prevent you from using the wrestler's escape demonstrated in technique 86 because he simply won't let go as you twist under him. Here, John demonstrates an alternative escape to reverse the top control. He will grab Jean Jacques's near (in this case, right) leg.

1 Jean Jacques is on top of John, grabbing around his torso. John is on all fours.

2 John steps out with his left leg and shoots his right leg forward, trying the wrestler's escape, but Jean Jacques is very strong and doesn't let go of the grip around John's chest.

3 John comes back with his head under Jean Jacques and reaches with his arms to grab Jean Jacques's right leg.

FIGHTING TECHNIQUES FIGHTING TECHNIQUES FIGHTING TECHNIQUES FIGHTING TECHN
ING TECHNIQUES FIGHTING TECHNIQUES FIGHTING TECHNIQUES FIGHTIN
ES FIGHTING TECHNIQUES FIGHTING TECHNIQUES FIGHTING TECHNIQUES
TECHNIQUES FIGHTING TECHNIQUES FIGHTING TECHNIQUES FIGHTING T
HTIN ES FIGHTING TECHNIQUES FIGH
IQUES TECHNIQUES FIGHTING TECHNIC

4 John grabs Jean Jacques's right leg with both arms and steps around with his left leg, ending up at a 90-degree angle to Jean Jacques. Jean Jacques still holds firmly around John's chest.

5 John reaches with his right hand and blocks Jean Jacques's left knee as he pushes off both legs, driving forward and forcing Jean Jacques to fall to the mat. Since Jean Jacques has locked his arms tightly around John and his left knee is blocked by John's right hand, he has no way to brace and stop his momentum. As he begins to fall to the mat, Jean Jacques lets go of his grip around John's torso in an attempt to block the fall but it is too late.

6 John ends up on top with both of Jean Jacques's legs together and in perfect position to pass the guard.

FIGHTING TECHNIQUES FIGHTING TECHNIQUES FIGHTING TECHNIQUES FIGHTING TECHNIQUES FIGHTING TECHNIQUES FIGHTING TECHNIQUES FIGHTING TECHNIQUES FIGHTING TECHNIQUES FIGHTING TECHNIQUES FIGHTING TECHNIQUE FIGHTING TECHNIQUES FIGHTING TECHNIQUES FIGHTING TECHNIQUES FIGHTING TECHNIQUES FIGHTING TE FIGHTING TECHNIQUES FIGHTING TECHNIQUES FIGHTING TECHNIQUES FIGHTING TECHNIQUES FIGHTING TECHNIQUES FIGHTING TECHNIQUES FIGHTING TECHNIQUES FIGHTING TECHNIQUES FIGHTING TECHNIQUES FIGHTING TECHNIQUES FIGHTING TECHNIQUES FIGHTING

88

Counter to the wrestler's escape from the mounted position

Dion attempts the wrestler's escape to the mount with John. John cleverly uses the same motion found in drill 7, circling the legs, to regain control of the situation; otherwise, Dion may end up on John's back or both on all fours. John then applies a neck crank for the submission. Note that neck cranks may not be allowed in certain tournaments (see restricted techniques in Article 6 of the IBJJF rules in the appendix), in which case—or simply as another option—John goes for a choke. The neck crank is the first option as it is quicker and doesn't require any more body movement.

1 John is mounted on Dion. Dion has his hands close together, protecting his neck, and his elbows pressing John's thighs, trying to prevent him from climbing up.

2 In a quick move—perhaps following an upa (bridge) escape or because of some space created by John's movement—Dion is able to slide his right arm inside John's left leg under the knee. Should John remain stationary, Dion will simply bridge to his left and drive his right arm around to his left, forcing John's leg over his head, thereby escaping from the mounted position and landing behind John.

3 As Dion bridges and starts the escape, John leaves his weight on his buttocks and pivots on Dion's chest while circling his left leg over the head.

4 Dion continues turning to his left. John continues to circle his leg, leaves his left leg open, and lands on Dion's side. Notice that John uses his weight to push against Dion's chest and his arms are open and ready to grab Dion's head.

5 John grabs Dion's head with both arms, clasping his right hand over his left. He drives his chest forward to trap Dion's right arm and leans back for the neck crank.

6 If neck cranks are not allowed (or as an alternative technique), John could plant his left arm out on the mat and circle his right arm in front of Dion's head while keeping his chest tight, trapping Dion's right arm.

7 John switches his legs, clasps his hands together, and applies the choking pressure by driving his chest forward and up, forcing Dion's right arm against his own neck. Pulling his arms tight completes the choke with John's right biceps against Dion's throat.

TING TECHNIQUES FIGHTING TECHNIQUES FIGHTING TECHNIQUES FIGHTI
ES FIGHTING TECHNIQUES FIGHTING TECHNIQUES FIGHTING TECHNIQUE
TECHNI FIGHTING TECHNIQUES FIGHTING TECHNIQUES FIGHTING TE
IGHTING TECHNIQUES FIGHTING TECHNIQUES FIGHTING TECHNIQUES FIG
NIQUES FIGHTING TECHNIQUES FIGHTING TECHNIQUES FIGHTING TECHNI
NG TECHNIQUES FIGHTING TECHNIQUES FIGHTING TECHNIQUES FIGHTING
NG TECHNIQUES FIGHTING TECHNIQUES FIGHTING TECHNIQUES FIGHTING

89

Counter to the wrestler's escape: submission variations 1

In this variation on the previous position, Dion was successful using the wrestler's escape and is struggling under John, keeping his right shoulder off the mat and making it very difficult for John to choke him. Some fighters are very strong and struggle with all their might. John does not want to fight for the submission as he may lose the side control and have Dion on all fours next to him, so he uses the following technique to score more points and to open up a couple of different submission opportunities.

1 John circles his legs and lands in side control on Dion. Dion is struggling to keep his right shoulder off the mat and is gaining ground toward turning to his knees. John grabs Dion's collar with his right hand and drives his forearm onto Dion's chin, keeping him from turning to his left.

2 John switches his legs, squares his hips, and slides his left knee over Dion's stomach. Notice that Dion's arms are trapped, so he cannot block John's knee from sliding. At this point, John can mount again and score 4 more points if he chooses to pause there for 3 seconds.

FIGHTING TECHNIQUES FIGHTING TECHNIQUES FIGHTING TECHNIQUES FIGHTING TECHN
ING TECHNIQUES FIGHTING TECHNIQUES FIGHTING TECHNIQUES FIGHTIN
ES FIGHTING TECHNIQUES FIGHTING TECHNIQUES FIGHTING TECHNIQUES
TECHNIQUES FIGHTING TECHNIQUES FIGHTING TECHNIQUES FIGHTING TI
HTIN QUES FIGHTING TECHNIQUES FIGH
IQUES G TECHNIQUES FIGHTING TECHNIC

3 John switches to the side mount, sliding his left knee near Dion's head, plants his left arm on the mat, and raises his right leg. John chokes Dion by driving his hips and right thigh up, forcing Dion's right arm against his own neck while John pulls his right elbow tight, driving his right forearm onto the opposite side of Dion's neck for the choke.

4 If he isn't confident that he can drive his hips forward on Dion without losing position, John will quickly change to an arm-lock. He starts out by shifting his weight back to his right and closing his right elbow to his right knee, trapping Dion's arm.

5 John continues sliding his right elbow over his right thigh, trapping Dion's right wrist with his right armpit. With his left arm, he pushes on Dion's face; simultaneously, he raises his hips while straightening his upper body for the armlock.

227

FIGHTING TECHNIQUES FIGHTING TECHNIQUES FIGHTING TECHNIQUES FIGHTI
UES FIGHTING TECHNIQUES FIGHTING TECHNIQUES FIGHTING TECHNIQUE
TECHNIQUES FIGHTING TECHNIQUES FIGHTING TECHNIQUES FIGHTING TE
FIGHTING TECHNIQUES FIGHTING TECHNIQUES FIGHTING TECHNIQUES FIG
NIQUES FIGHTING TECHNIQUES FIGHTING TECHNIQUES FIGHTING TECHNIC
ING TECHNIQUES FIGHTING TECHNIQUES FIGHTING TECHNIQUES FIGHTING

90

Counter to the wrestler's escape: submission variations 2

Here, John attempts the previous submission (the straight-up armlock), but the cagey Dion continues to anticipate and escape. He was able to evade John's wrist trap and has foiled the armlock attempt by twisting his wrist and bringing the forearm down. John, however, has a few more submission options ready at his disposal. This is another example of Jean Jacques and John's theory of having small connected circles of moves. By mastering the following options, you will have an arsenal of submissions from this position that will force even the most experience fighter to fall into a submission. It is extremely important to perfect the timing of these submissions. By practicing the attacks in sequence with a willing partner, you will be able to fluidly change from one submission to another until your opponent falls prey to one. Again, repetition and practice will cut milliseconds from your execution time and greatly increase your rate of success.

1 John attempts a straight-up arm bar on Dion.

2 Dion quickly reacts to escape the submission by twisting his wrist and bringing his forearm down. John quickly steps over Dion's head with his left leg while maintaining his left-hand pressure on Dion's chest or face. With his right hand, John grabs Dion's right sleeve to keep him from turning in any direction. Note that John uses his left arm brace on Dion's chest to help raise his body and pivot his hips, making it easy for him to get his left leg over Dion's head.

3 John falls back to the mat and straightens Dion's arm for the armlock.

4 Another option John likes is to go for the tri- angle. Again, Dion's arm is somewhat free. John grabs Dion's collar with his right hand as far in as possible.

5 As Dion uses his left arm to try to defend the attack, John quickly intercepts it, grabs Dion's arm with his right hand, and steps over it with his right leg, placing his heel right next to Dion's head.

6 John grabs the back of Dion's head with his left hand and, while still keeping control of the right wrist with his own right hand, spins his body to his left and sits on the mat, bringing Dion's head up.

7 John circles his left leg around and locks it over his right foot for the figure-four triangle around Dion's head.

FIGHTING TECHNIQUES FIGHTING TECHNIQUES

91

Escaping from the biceps cutter and counter options

The biceps cutter is a devastating submission that can cause significant damage. Athletes with high pain tolerance will ignore the pain caused by the submission and end up with a nasty broken arm. Although the biceps cutter is illegal in many tournaments (see restricted techniques in Article 6 of the IBJJF rules in the appendix), it is important to know how to escape it, because you may encounter it in some competitions or in training. Here, John first demonstrates a defense, then shows a couple of submission options.

1 John is passing Dion's guard and gets caught in a biceps cutter lock. Notice that Dion's left shin is pressing against John's right biceps, and he has locked a figure-four with his right leg over his left foot, trapping John's forearm. Should John continue to pass to Dion's right or do nothing, he will have to submit. Dion will apply the pressure by using both his hands behind John's right triceps while stretching his legs, pressing against John's biceps. Notice that John has his right knee up and left knee down because he was attempting to reach Dion's side and pass the guard to Dion's right.

2 John starts his defense by moving back to his own right—away from the pressure. He kneels down with his right knee and scoots his body back to center.

3 He then steps to his right and drives his right knee next to his right forearm, forcing it in the gap between his forearm and Dion's right thigh, and creating a space to pull his right arm out.

FIGHTING TECHNIQUES FIGHTING TECHNIC FIGHTING TECHNIQUES FIGHTING TECHNIQUES FIGHTING TECHNIQUES FIGHTING TECHNIQUES FIGHTING

4 Once he has released the pressure of the biceps cutter, John falls back to the mat. His right knee still pushes against Dion's leg. Notice that at this point John has trapped Dion's right leg with his own right elbow pressing against his right knee.

5 John falls back to the mat, circles his right arm around Dion's right heel, locking it in the crease of his elbow, clasps his hands together, and applies a heel hook by twisting the ankle counterclockwise. Note that the heel hook is illegal in some Brazilian jiu-jitsu competitions. In that case, you can use the following straight footlock option.

6 Straight footlock option: John wraps his right arm around Dion's right ankle, locking his right hand on his left forearm to create a tight hold. John places his left hand on Dion's shin, brings his knees together, trapping Dion's right leg and blocking him from coming up, and applies the footlock pressure by arching back with his torso. Notice that Dion's foot is locked under John's right armpit. As John arches back, he drives the front part of the foot down for the submission, applying great pressure on the ankle joint.

TING TECHNIQUES FIGHTING TECHNIQUES FIGHTING TECHNIQUES FIGHTI
UES FIGHTING TECHNIQUES FIGHTING TECHNIQUES FIGHTING TECHNIQUE
TECHNI FIGHTING TECHNIQUES FIGHTING TECHNIQUES FIGHTING TE
FIGHTING TECHNIQUES FIGHTING TECHNIQUES FIGHTING TECHNIQUES FI
NIQUE TECHNIQUES FIGHTING TECHNIQUES FIGHTING TECHNIQUES FIGHTING TECHNIC
ING TECHNIQUES FIGHTING TECHNIQUES FIGHTING TECHNIQUES FIGHTING

92

Escaping from the omoplata to footlock

Every athlete gets caught in a dangerous position at some point; being able to defend properly (and even come back with a submission counter) will not only save you from a submission but may also win a match that appeared to be lost. In technique 91, John demonstrated an escape and counter to the biceps cutter and gave you two submission options. Here, John shows you how to defend the omoplata (shoulder lock) and gives you more submissions as well.

The omoplata is a common, effective, and adaptable submission technique. Expect good guard players to attack the shoulder with different approaches—all ending in the omoplata. The key to any defense and counter is to be aware of the submission attempt early and apply the defense right away. Knowing one good escape and applying it quickly will yield better results than knowing many and taking too long to decide which one is best. By the time you decide, you may already be tapping!

1 John got caught in an omoplata when Dion circled his left leg around John's right arm and locked the figure-four around the shoulder while trapping the forearm with his hips. If John doesn't react properly, Dion will sit up and apply torque to John's shoulder for the submission.

2 Reverse Angle

2 John's first reaction is to defend the lock! He grabs his own belt with his right hand, thus preventing Dion from driving his arm around the shoulder joint. He then steps forward with his left foot and raises his torso. The lock is now defended at least temporarily. If John doesn't do anything, Dion will try to break John's grip on his belt to continue the submission. With his left hand, John grabs Dion's right foot by the toes . . .

3 And drives the foot down toward his own hips.

4 John turns his body to his right as he presses Dion's foot in for the footlock.

5 If Dion's right leg is high, John drives his head under Dion's calf and pulls down on Dion's toes for the footlock.

TING TECHNIQUES FIGHTING TECHNIQUES FIGHTING TECHNIQUES FIGHTI
UES FIGHTING TECHNIQUES FIGHTING TECHNIQUES FIGHTING TECHNIQUE
TECHNI   FIGHTING TECHNIQUES FIGHTING TECHNIQUES FIGHTING TE
FIGHTING TECHNIQUES FIGHTING TECHNIQUES FIGHTING TECHNIQUES FI
NIQUES   TECHNIQUES FIGHTING TECHNIQUES FIGHTING TECHNI
ING TECHNIQUES FIGHTING TECHNIQUES FIGHTING TECHNIQUES FIGHTING

93

Escaping from the sitting guard and counter

The sitting guard and its variations are very tough to deal with, especially in the case where your opponent sits up, trapping one of your legs, and grabs either the sleeve or the belt. Here John achieves good position, Jean Jacques uses a very effective escape, and John goes one step further by following the escape with a counter takedown. Notice that John's move for the counter takedown is the same as drill 3, coming up to your knee.

1 John is in the sitting guard, trapping Jean Jacques's left leg with his right arm. Notice how John's left foot blocks Jean Jacques's right foot from moving forward and his left hand holds Jean Jacques's right knee. From here, John can apply a variety of sweeps, so Jean Jacques needs to escape quickly.

2 Jean Jacques pushes John back with his left hand as he pivots on his left foot and turns.

3 Jean Jacques turns his back on John completely and walks away. As John still holds Jean Jacques's left leg, Jean Jacques kicks his left leg forward to escape John's grip.

FIGHTING TECHNIQUES FIGHTING TECHNIQUES FIGHTING TECHNIQUES FIGHTING TECHNIQUES FI
NIQUES FIGHTING TECHNIQUES FIGHTING TECHNIQUES FIGHTING TECHNI
ING TECHNIQUES FIGHTING TECHNIQUES FIGHTING TECHNIQUES FIGHTIN
ES FIGHTING TECHNIQUES FIGHTING TECHNIQUES FIGHTING TECHNIQUES
TECHNIQUES FIGHTING TECHNIQUES FIGHTING TECHNIQUES FIGHTING TE
GHTING TECHNIQUES FIGHTING TECHNIQUES FIGHTING TECHNIQUES FIGH
NIQUES FIGHTING TECHNIQUES FIGHTING TECHNIQUES FIGHTING TECHNIC

4 Anticipating that Jean Jacques will kick his leg and escape, John lets go of the leg, tucks his left leg in, leans forward (drill 3), and reaches to grab Jean Jacques's legs.

5 John springs forward off his feet and launches himself at Jean Jacques, grabbing both ankles with his hands in a claw grip (four fingers and thumb together). It is very important to use this grip because the claw possesses much more power than the normal grip with the thumb on the opposite side. It will also protect you from breaking your thumb as you lunge to get the opponents' legs.

6 As John blocks Jean Jacques's ankles, Jean Jacques's forward momentum away from John forces him to fall on the mat.

FIGHTING TECHNIQUES FIGHTING TECHNIQUES FIGHTING TECHNIQUES FIGHTING TECHNIQUES FIGHTING TECHNIQUES FIGHTING TECHNIQUES FIGHTING TECHNIQUES FIGHTING TECHNIQUES FIGHTING TECHNIQUES FIGHTING TE FIGHTING TECHNIQUES FIGHTING TECHNIQUES FIGHTING TECHNIQUES FIGHTING TECHNIQUES FI NIQUES FIGHTING TECHNIQUES FIGHTING TECHNIQUES FIGHTING TECHNI ING TECHNIQUES FIGHTING TECHNIQUES FIGHTIN

94

Escaping the leg grab: shoulder lock or triangle

It is common for an opponent to gain control of your leg by wrapping his arms around it as he prepares for a takedown. In technique 93, Jean Jacques demonstrated the kick-out escape where he either turned and walked away from John or simply kicked his trapped leg out. In this case, however, John is not sitting but rather is up on his knees, allowing him to spring to his feet quickly and follow Jean Jacques's evasive action. If Jean Jacques turns and tries to walk away, John can quickly get up, continue holding the leg, and apply a trip takedown. So Jean Jacques opts for a variation of the triangle.

1 Jean Jacques is standing with his right leg trapped by John. John has both his arms wrapped around the leg and is on his knees, trying to bring Jean Jacques down. Jean Jacques demonstrates good posture with his right knee bent forward pushing against John's chest. This serves two purposes: 1) if Jean Jacques allows his leg to be straightened, he will fall back because John will simply pull the shin back while applying pressure to the knee, and 2) the position both forces John back and enables Jean Jacques to keep a good base.

2 Since John is kneeling and does not have his legs on the ground as in the previous technique, Jean Jacques can easily circle his right leg out from inside John's legs. As he does so, he circles his right foot around John's left knee until it is outside the thigh.

3 Jean Jacques plants his right foot firmly on the mat next to John's left thigh. He continues to drive his right knee forward, but because his foot is outside, it slides from John's chest between his arm and chest. Jean Jacques assists the move by pulling John's left elbow up with his right hand. Without Jean Jacques's right knee blocking his chest, John's body moves forward and he thinks he can take Jean Jacques down.

NIQUES FIGHTING TECHNIQUES FIGHTING TECHNIQUES FIGHTING TECHNIQUES FIGHTING TECHN
TING TECHNIQUES FIGHTING TECHNIQUES FIGHTING TECHNIQUES FIGHTING TECHN
ES FIGHTING TECHNIQUES FIGHTING TECHNIQUES FIGHTING TECHNIQUES
TECHNIQUES FIGHTING TECHNIQUES FIGHTING TECHNIQUES FIGHTING TI
GHTIN TECHNIQUES FIGHTING TECHNIQUES FIGH
NIQUES TECHNIQ

4 Jean Jacques baits John into the takedown as he falls backwards and loops his left leg up onto John's right shoulder. With his left hand, Jean Jacques grabs John's gi on the back of the neck. To break John's posture and to help get his leg over John's right shoulder, Jean Jacques falls back while pulling on John's gi collar.

4 Detail (incorrect technique) If Jean Jacques doesn't grab the back of John's gi with his left hand, but instead uses both hands on the arm, John can simply pull his torso and head back, keeping good posture and negating Jean Jacques's triangle.

5 As he hits the mat with his back, Jean Jacques has his left leg over John's right arm on his shoulder and is ready for the triangle. His right foot is off the mat and loops around John's back, trapping the left arm and head inside.

6 Jean Jacques pulls John's left elbow toward his head with both hands for a shoulder lock. If John manages to release his left arm and bring it around to escape the shoulder lock, he will be in the triangle!

FIGHTING TECHNIQUES FIGHTING TECHNIQUES FIGHTING TECHNIQUES FIGHTING TECHN
ING TECHNIQUES FIGHTING TECHNIQUES FIGHTING TECHNIQUES FIGHTING TECHNI
JES FIGHTING TECHNIQUES FIGHTING TECHNIQUES FIGHTING TECHNIQUE
TECHNI FIGHTING TECHNIQUES FIGHTING TECHNIQUES FIGHTING TE
FIGHTING TECHNIQUES FIGHTING TECHNIQUES FIGHTING TECHNIQUES FIG
NIQUES FIGHTING TECHNIQUES FIGHTING TECHNIQUES FIGHTING TECHNIC
NG TECHNIQUES FIGHTING TECHNIQUES FIGHTING TECHNIQUES FIGHTING

95

Counter to omoplata escape

One of the common ways to escape the omoplata is simply to roll forward over your head, removing the attacker's ability to torque your arm around the shoulder joint. In this demonstration, John attempts that escape, knowing that rolling forward will bring him to his back and cost him the 2-point sweep, but hoping that he will avoid submission. Jean Jacques, however, likes to submit, and once he gets a good position he always has options ready to use. In this case, he blocks John's escape route and applies a different submission.

1 Jean Jacques has caught John in the omoplata (shoulder lock). He has a figure-four lock with his legs around John's right arm and plans to sit up to apply pressure on John's shoulder. John's defense is to roll forward over his head, removing Jean Jacques's ability to torque his shoulder.

2 Sensing John's escape, Jean Jacques drops his right leg down below John's shin . . .

3 And locks it under John's shin, negating John's ability to roll forward. At the same time, Jean Jacques stretches the legs, forcing John's shoulder down while pushing his face up.

4 Jean Jacques pulls John's right arm away with both hands . . .

5 And lifts and pushes it against his left calf, applying pressure on the elbow for the armlock.

APPENDIX

IBJJF (International Brazilian Jiu-Jitsu Federation) Rules

Article 1: Area of Competition

The stage on which the competition will take place will be composed of 2 or more fighting areas, surrounded by all the supporting assistants, referees, timekeepers, inspectors, security personnel, and a disciplinary department summoned by the coordinators, with the power to punish any unethical conduct of coaches, teachers, referees, or other assistants that might interfere in the progress of the event.

Fighting Areas: Each area (ring) must be composed of a minimum of 32 tatames (mats), a total of 51.84 square meters. This area will be divided into two areas: the inner area, composed of at least 18 tatames of a green color, and the outer (safety) area, composed of 14 yellow tatames (or any other color other than green).

Article 2: Equipment

The Directing Table: The table that coordinates and directs the tasks and positions at the competition, at which will remain the announcer/controller of the event and the competent authority, will be placed in front of each ring. Parallel to the directing table are chairs for the referees and a note-taker. Only they may occupy these chairs. Beside the referees' chairs is a chair occupied by the inspector of the refereeing. It is the inspector's duty to make sure that the refereeing runs smoothly, as well as to inspect the credentials of the competing athletes.

Scoreboards: Each area of competition is to have two scoreboards, indicating a count horizontally, situated on the outside of the directing table, easily viewed by the referee, commission, and spectators.

Chairs, banners, and tables are to be placed strategically to the side of the area of competition for the best assessment of each match.

Stopwatches are mandatory for keeping track of the duration of the matches and the reserve time.

Article 3: Refereeing

The mat referee is the highest authority on the mat and has the authority to disqualify competitors during the match. No one can change his decision. In special cases the IBJJF can review and overturn a referee's decision if the decision is unjust. The referee is assisted by the timekeeper in the matches. In cases where a referee shows himself incapable to continue refereeing because of obvious mistakes, the inspector of the event has the authority to replace him.

During the match the central referee is to be always directing the competitors to the center of the ring. In the event that the competitors move out of bounds during the match, the referee will call stop and the competitors are to hold their position without movement. The same occurrence will happen when two-thirds of the body is outside the boundary. The referee may be assisted by the timekeeper in moving the athletes back to the center of the ring. In case the referee and timekeeper are unable to move the athletes back to the center of the ring, the athletes will be asked to walk back to the center and continue from the same position.

The referee will not allow interference from outsiders during the match. A medical team or nurse will be allowed on the mat at the referee's discretion.

During the match the referee or persons at the scoring table are not allowed to converse with the competitors; this will be strictly enforced.

Expiration of time will be determined by the timekeeper during the match. The timekeeper will notify the central referee immediately with an auditory and visual signal.

After the table gives the signal whistle that the match is over, the referee can give an advantage point to the combatant for attempting a submission or for attempting to establish a dominant position without maintaining it for the precise time, except for takedowns, for which one doesn't need to establish a dominant position to earn points.

The judge's table will record the referee's gestures on a scorecard. The table will have two official scoreboards with green, yellow, and white cards for scoring the points and advantages.

Notes taken are the responsibility of the scorekeepers. Notes may not be altered and must be exactly what the central referee dictates.

Important: Any and every situation that cannot be determined by the manual will be left up to the referee's discretion.

Position and Function of the Central Referee

The central referee is to remain in the area of combat, directing the combat, determining the results, and certifying the correct decisions in registration placement.

The central referee is to give the first athlete on the mat a green-and-yellow belt for identification in case the athletes' kimonos are the same colors. The referee may also require the athlete to don the green-and-yellow belt at his discretion.

The throwing techniques of the competitors, by order of the central referee, will be noted on the scoreboard or on the official score papers by the scorekeeper with only the corresponding points. In case of a draw in points and advantages, the scorekeeper will raise the two flags together simultaneously. Then the central referee will analyze who was the fighter with the better performance in accordance with the rules and award the victory to the fighter determined to be most aggressive in pursuing the victory during the fight. There will be no draws in any case. The central referee will decide who is the winner and his decision is absolute.

The central referee will oversee that everything is correct, including the ring, equipment, gis, hygiene, officials, and all other matters before starting the fight.

The referee must certify that no one—not the public, not photographers, nor anyone else—occupies any position that could interfere, risk, or harm the competitors.

Gi Checker

The gi checker verifies before the fight that the color and condition of each competitor's belt is appropriate, that the competitors' nails are trimmed, and that their gis are correctly fitted by the official IBJJF measuring tool.

Article 4: Gestures

The central referee will make gestures indicated below, according with the actions:

For all gestures made, the central referee will raise his hand indicating the athlete receiving the score with his armband in accordance with the color of the athlete's colored gi or indicating belt.

Takedowns, sweeps, and knee-on-belly: The referee will raise his hand indicating the scoring athlete's color and the score of 2 points.

Passing the guard: The referee will raise his hand indicating the scoring athlete's color and the score of 3 points.

Front mount, back mount, and back grab: The referee will raise his hand indicating the scoring athlete's color and the score of 4 points.

Penalties: The referee will signal the color of the penalized competitor, turn his hands one over the other (circle) with both fists, and give an advantage to the other fighter.

Advantages: The referee signals advantages with arm extended, sweeping outward on a horizontal plane level with the shoulder.

For the interruption of the fight: The referee opens his arms together on a horizontal plane level with the shoulder.

For interruption of time during the fight: The referee puts his hands one above the other forming a "T", signaling the timekeeper to stop the time.

Article 5: Fighting Conclusions

There is never a draw. Bouts will be decided by:
  1. Submission
  2. Disqualification

3. Unconsciousness
4. Points
5. Advantages

1. Submission

Submission occurs when a technique forces an opponent into admitting defeat by:

A. Tapping with the palm against his opponent or the floor in a visible manner,

B. Tapping with his feet on the ground (if he is unable to use his hands),

C. Requesting verbally to the referee that the fight be stopped (if he can't tap with his hands or his feet), or

D. Requesting that the fight be ended if the athlete gets injured or feels physically incapable or unprepared.

Also:

E. The referee may end the fight, giving victory to the athlete who applied the lock, if the referee sees a lock being properly applied and is certain that the other athlete is exposed to serious physical damage.

F. A coach of one of the athletes may request that the fight be ended either by directing himself to the referee or by throwing the towel into the ring for any reason.

G. The referee may end the fight when one of the athletes is injured or by doctor's examination proving he is incapable to continue. If this occurs, the victory will be given to the opponent as long as the injury was not caused intentionally by conduct worthy of disqualification.

2. Disqualification

Serious Fouls

Serious fouls are those that lead to immediate disqualification by the referee. The following circumstances warrant the penalty of a serious foul and disqualification:

1. The use of foul language, cursing, or other immoral acts of disrespect toward the referee or any of the assisting public.

2. Biting, hair pulling, putting fingers into the eyes or nose of one's opponent, intentionally seeking to injure genitalia, or the use of fists, feet, knees, elbows, or heads with the intention to hurt or gain unfair advantage.

3. When a fighter has his kimono ripped during a fight, the referee will give him a set time to change it. If the fighter does not change it in time, he will be disqualified.

4. Fighters must wear shorts under the pants, keeping in mind the risk that the suit might be torn or unsewn. If this occurs, the athlete will be given a set time determined by the referee to find another pair of

pants to wear. If the athlete cannot change within the set time, he will be immediately disqualified.

5. If an athlete has been submitted to a lock and runs out of the ring to avoid tapping out, he will be immediately disqualified. If it is considered a technical foul rather than a disciplinary foul, the offender may still fight other matches in the tournament.

Lesser Fouls (Penalties)

The following circumstances warrant penalties:

1. The athlete kneels without first having gripped his opponent's kimono.
2. When either of the athletes runs to one of the edges of the ring to avoid combat, or while groundfighting flees by crawling or rolling out of the ring or by standing up, thereby avoiding engaging, or purposely stepping out of the ring to gain time.
3. When, in order to allow himself rest or to avoid attacks, an athlete takes off his kimono or allows it to be taken off with the intention of stopping the fight.
4. When an athlete inserts his fingers inside his opponent's sleeves or pants, or uses both his hands on his opponent's belt.
5. When an athlete deliberately stalls the fight, including standing up or holding his adversary when in the guard, on top, or on bottom without seeking to engage or gain submissions. Noticing this, the referee will request that 30 seconds be marked. If the athlete does not change his position or show visible signs of engagement within 30 seconds, he will lose 2 points and both athletes will return to their feet at neutral positions. The same will happen on the second offence, with the possibility of disqualification on the third offence.

Note: A penalty with immediate loss of 2 points occurs when an athlete runs from the ring in order to avoid a sweep that the referee considers would have been completed, or when an athlete flees the ring in order to avoid a lock that has not yet been completed (fleeing a lock that has been completed results in disqualification—see item 5 under "Serious Fouls" above).

- On the **first offence** the offender will be given a verbal warning.
- On the **second offence** the offender's opponent will be given an advantage.
- On the **third offence** the offender's opponent will be given 2 points.
- **After the third offence** the referee may disqualify the athlete for any further fouls.

3. Unconsciousness

One of the two opponents is defeated after losing consciousness by any of the following valid moves: strangling, pressuring, takedowns, or accidents in which the adversary has not committed any foul worthy of disqualification.

4. Points

The competition makes the athletes use their technical abilities in attempting to finish or neutralize their opponents. Points are awarded for technical superiority displayed during the match. To attain a point the athlete needs to control the position for 3 seconds.

Important: An athlete who has received points for a position will not generate new points by changing positions intentionally and returning to the first position. For example, no new points will be awarded for the knee-on-belly position, then switching sides and applying the knee-on-belly on the opposite side.

No points will be marked for the athlete who is attaining a position while in a submission. Points will only be awarded after the submission is completely defended. For example, when one athlete is mounted on his opponent but is in a guillotine, the points of the mount will be awarded only when the submission is defended.

A. Takedowns: Any kind of knocking or taking the opponent down on his backside, *2 points.* If the athlete is thrown to the ground and does not land on his back, the thrower must pin him to the ground in the same position for at least 3 seconds to gain the points for the takedown.

Observation 1: The takedown that lands outside of the fighting area and in the security area will be valid as long as the athlete that applied it stood with both feet in the fighting area while making the takedown.

Observation 2: If the athlete has one of his knees on the ground and is taken down, whoever applied the takedown will be awarded 2 points as long as he had both his feet on the ground. If the athlete has both his knees on the ground and is knocked down, the standing athlete will have to pass to his side and maintain this position to receive an advantage.

Observation 3: When the athlete attempts the double-leg takedown and the opponent sits on the floor and executes a sweep, the athlete who attempted the takedown will not receive points but the one who executed the sweep will.

Observation 4: When a competitor throws his opponent and ends up in a bottom position, the competitor executing the throw will receive 2 points and the opponent on top will receive an advantage. If the competitor executing the throw lands in his opponent's guard and is swept, both will receive 2 points.

B. Passing the guard: The athlete who is above his adversary and between his legs moves to his opponent's side and thereby establishes a perpendicular or longitudinal position over his adversary's trunk—dominating him and leaving him no space to move or to escape the position, *3 points.* Three points are awarded regardless of whether the athlete underneath is on his side, back, or facing down.

Note: If the athlete underneath avoids the move by getting to his knees or standing up, the initiative will not be awarded 3 points but will be awarded an advantage.

C. Knee-on-belly: The athlete on top across-side places one knee on his adversary's stomach, with his other leg slightly flexed and that foot planted on the ground, and holds his collar or sleeve and belt, *2 points.*

Observation: If the athlete underneath prevents his adversary from bringing his knee down onto the belly or if the one on top does not establish the position completely or has his open leg foot planted on the ground, the move will not be awarded with 2 points but will be awarded an advantage.

D. The mount: The athlete sits on his opponent's torso (the opponent can be lying on his stomach, side, or back), *4 points.* The one mounted can be on top of one of his opponent's arms but never on both. It will also be considered a mount if he has one knee and one foot on the ground.

Observation: No points will be awarded if the feet or knees of the athlete on top are not on the ground but on his opponent's leg. Also, if an athlete applies a triangle while in the guard and in so doing lands mounted on his opponent, the move will be considered a sweep not a mount. (See passing the guard, above)

E. The back grab: The athlete takes his adversary's back and, wrapping his legs around his opponent's waist, with his heels hooking the inner side of his opponent's thighs, prohibits him from leaving the position, *4 points.*

Note: The points will not be awarded if both heels are not properly positioned on the inner part of the adversary's thighs. The back grab is still considered if the attacker has one of his legs over the adversary's arm but not over both.

F. The sweep: The athlete underneath has his opponent in his guard (between his legs) or in the half-guard (having one of his adversary's legs between his) and is able to get on top of his adversary by inverting his position, *2 points.*

Observation 1: It will not be consider a sweep if the move does not begin from inside the guard or half-guard.

Observation 2: When the athlete sweeping advances his position to the back of his opponent during the attempted sweep, he is awarded 2 points.

Observation 3: An athlete will be awarded 2 points if he starts in guard, attempts a sweep, both athletes return to their feet, and the competitor attempting the sweep executes a takedown and remains on top.

5. Advantages

It is considered an advantage when the athlete attempts but does not complete any of the fundamental moves of the fight.

- If one of the athletes attempts a technique, it is up to the referee to decide whether he will award an advantage.
- Advantages will be awarded during standing fighting if an athlete attempts a technique with more aggressiveness and initiative, trying takedowns or other finalizing moves during the fight.

- Advantages will be awarded during ground fighting if an athlete attempts a technique and puts his adversary on the defensive.
- Advantages will be awarded for attempted takedowns when an athlete causes his opponent to visibly lose balance. A visible loss of balance during an attempted throw will also result in an advantage.
- Advantages will be awarded during the closed guard (the athlete on the bottom has his legs wrapped around his opponent's waist) accordingly:
  - A. The one on top will earn the advantage by being on the offensive, trying to dominate his adversary's guard (pass the guard). For the referee to award an advantage, the athlete on top must come close to passing the guard, forcing his adversary to exert energy to regain position (for example, forcing the half-guard, almost immobilizing, etc.).
  - B. The one underneath will earn the advantage if he almost sweeps his opponent, putting him in a dangerous position, as well as if he attempts a lock that forces his opponent to defend.
  Note: For the sweep attempt to be considered worthy of an advantage, the athlete underneath must open his own legs in an attempt to come over the top.
  - C. In the case of an athlete attempting to pass the guard who attempts a footlock without success with the adversary sitting up, the competitor on top will receive an advantage point. In addition, a competitor who attempts a submission and puts his opponent in visible danger will receive an advantage point.

Article 6: Restrictions

In all categories the central referee has the authority to stop a match when either of the competitors is in danger of serious bodily harm as a result of a submission, and to award the victory to the competitor applying the submission.

- Cervical locks and neck cranks are disallowed without exception in all categories. Competitors attempting a cervical lock will receive no warnings but will be immediately disqualified.
- Athletes under 18 are only allowed to compete in the open class if they are middleweight or heavier.
- Any clothing or gear that can alter the outcome of a match in any way is disallowed in competition. This includes headgear, shirts under the gi, any kind of protectors, and wrestling or other shoes.
- In children's divisions (4–15 years), when a competitor is executing a triangle and the opponent stands up, it is the referee's obligation to stand in a position to protect both athletes, specifically to reduce the risk of spinal damage.

Restricted Techniques: Ages 4 to 12

Knee lock, leg lock
Footlock (of any kind)
Calf lock
Omoplata (shoulder lock)
Biceps lock
Frontal *mata leão*
Bate estaca

Cervical lock (any kind)
Mao de vaca
Triangle pulling the head
Ezekiel
Technical frontal tie (guillotine)
Heel hook

Restricted Techniques: Ages 13 to 15

Bate estaca
Biceps lock
Mao de vaca
Triangle pulling the head
Footlock (any kind)
Knee lock, leg lock
Cervical lock (any kind)

Frontal *mata leão*
Ezekiel
Calf lock
Kanibasami (scissor takedown)
Heel hook

Restricted Techniques: Ages 16 to 17

Bate estaca
Leg locks
Cervical lock
Biceps lock
Calf lock

Mao de vaca
Mata leão with foot
Kanibasami (scissor takedown)
Heel hook

Restricted Techniques: Adult through Senior— Blue & Purple Belt

Mata leão with foot
Bate estaca
Leg locks
Cervical lock
Biceps lock
Calf lock
Kanibasami (scissor takedown)
Heel hook

Restricted Techniques: Adult through Senior— Brown & Black Belt

Biceps lock
Cervical lock
Kanibasami (scissor takedown)
Heel hook

Article 7: Hygiene

Competitors must abide by the following hygiene specifications in order to compete:
A. The kimono must be washed and dried and free of all unpleasant odors.
B. Toenails and fingernails must be cut short and clean.
C. Persons with long hair must keep their hair from interfering with their opponent or themselves during the match.
D. Athletes are not permitted to paint their hair with spray and may be disqualified by the referee for doing so.

Article 8: Kimono

Competitors are required to wear kimonos and must abide by the following kimono specifications in order to compete:
A. Kimonos are to be constructed of cotton or similar material and in good condition. The material may not be excessively thick or hard to the point that it will obstruct the opponent.
B. Colors may be white or blue. No combined colors (i.e., white kimono with blue pants).
C. The jacket is to be of sufficient length down to the thighs; sleeves must reach the wrist with arms extended in front of the body.
D. Belt width is to be between 4 and 5 centimeters, with color corresponding to rank, and tied around the waist tight enough to keep the kimono closed.
E. Athletes are not permitted to compete with torn kimonos, sleeves that are not of proper length or with t-shirts underneath the kimono (except in female divisions).

Article 9: Fight Durations

Age 4 to 6: 2 minutes
Age 7 to 9: 3 minutes
Age 10 to 15: 4 minutes
Age 16 to 18: 5 minutes
Adult
White: 5 minutes
Blue: 6 minutes
Purple: 7 minutes
Brown: 8 minutes
Black: 10 minutes
Master
Blue: 5 minutes
Purple: 6 minutes
Brown: 6 minutes
Black: 6 minutes

Senior
Blue: 5 minutes
Purple: 5 minutes
Brown: 5 minutes
Black: 5 minutes

5 x 5 Team Championship Times
Men
Blue: 6 minutes
Purple: 7 minutes
Brown and black: 10 minutes
Women
Blue: 6 minutes
Purple, brown, and black: 7 minutes

Article 10: Direction and Decision

1. All those serving as officials in the competition, including as technicians, professors, directors, timekeepers, or in other capacity—are subject to punishment by the enforcing body for any illegal actions. Other unofficial persons who give instructions from inside the dedicated area of competition will warrant disqualification of the competitor.

2. In the case that both athletes are accidentally injured and unable to continue during the final match, the scorecard will determine the result.

    A. If points or advantages are confirmed, they will determine the winner.

    B. If no points or advantages exist, the result will be a draw.

3. If the two athletes start from a position on the ground in any situation, the decision will be made as if they had started from a standing position.

4. In final matches there will be a maximum of two rest periods.

5. For the final match the competitors will be allowed two opportunities to make weight.

6. If one of the competitors does not appear for the final match, the athlete present will be awarded the win and the absent competitor will not receive a medal.